IDOL SCRIBBLINGS

Deities Ancient and Modern For All Occasions

By

Hannah Hudson~Lee

First published in Great Britain in 2019 by Idol Reads

© Hannah Hudson-Lee 2019

Hannah Hudson-Lee has asserted her right under the Copyright, Designs and Patents Act 1988 to be identified as the author of this work.

This book is sold subject to the condition that it shall not, by way of trade or otherwise, be lent, resold, hired out, or otherwise circulated without the publisher's prior consent and without a similar condition being imposed upon the subsequent purchaser. No part of this publication may be reproduced without the publisher's prior consent. This book must not be circulated in any form of binding or cover other than that which is published and without a similar condition being placed on the subsequent purchaser.

ISBN 978-1-9162911-0-2

Printed in and bound in Great Britain by John Brailsford Printers, Rotherham, S62 6EU.

Typesetting by Kristian Hudson-Lee

INTRODUCTION

This introduction should probably be highbrow. It should probably make some statement about considering what western polytheism might be like in the modern age. It should probably pay tribute to the ancient cultures that it draws upon. It could make a statement about modern Paganism. However, that would be entirely inappropriate as this is an extremely silly book.

It all started one cold day in early May 2018, when the UK was being blasted by an unseasonal "Beast from the East" weather system. Stuck inside, sheltering from a surgical wind, my friends and I were passing the time by playing silly games of our own invention via social media. In one such game, originally called #CreateADeity, I invited my friends to suggest Gods and Goddesses that don't exist, but that we probably need in our modern lives.

Some of the ideas that came up were pure genius. I like doodling, and so I started to render some of the suggested characters as cartoons to amuse the players. I would also try to develop a bit of back story for each God and their following. These proved extremely popular with my friends, and they suggested that I turn them into the book you now hold. I hope that you have as much fun reading this book as we have had creating it. Please see the "With Thanks" page for a list of everyone involved in the "Hive Mind".

Idol Scribblings is also available through my blog with new deities posted every week. Come and have a look at

https://IdolScribblings.blog

Oh, and if you were about to be offended, please remember….
All deities in this book are entirely fictional and any resemblance to Gods, Goddesses, Persons or Civilizations living or dead is purely co-incidental. I have not been smitten yet, so it's all probably fine.

This book is dedicated to…

Every one in **The Idol Scribbling Hive Mind** especially Kris Hudson Lee, Teresa Lee, Mike Lee and Janet Hudson.

FOREWORD
By Dr Gareth Wilden

In my humble opinion, Ms. Hudson-Lee is the best author of alternative Scottish future erotic camel racing fiction in the world. While I would be delighted to write the foreword for the 27th instalment in the Dougal Al-Badawi trilogy, this is unfortunately not that book. Sadly, we will have to wait a little longer to find out how Bunty three-humps is rescued from the industrial vat of haggis soup and makes it to Mars in time for the Olympus Mons Oaks, but I digress.

Or rather let me regress. To this book, and the start of it. Where did it start from? Well, where does any idea start from these days? Let's refine that a little - where does any BAD idea start from? These days, the unholy trinity of bad ideas tends to consist of alcohol, bad puns, and social media. It was a what-if, or a how-about, or a couldn't-we or a why-not, the origins of which are lost in the mists of binary archives past (but can still be found on Hannah's time line; or the NSA backup thereof) from whence the first of these Gods appeared. Undaunted from first steps, the project bloomed and blossomed, and Hannah suddenly taking the joke seriously, producing more and more content and taking up art classes to improve the iconography portrayed. One of the joys of this series has been watching Hannah's art develop and progress: the sarcasm and pathos needed no encouragement.

But what of the subject material? Well, let's begin at the beginning. Where a God created the world (and I will use term God here as a generalisation as unbelievably, wars continue to start over this point). But from that start Gods and Goddesses multiplied in all directions - with over seven thousand religions known and no two sharing the same Gods. Indeed, the explosion of religion, and thus godhood, into every niche in the growing world neatly espouses Darwinism evolution (that many of them would decry) to fill every ecological niche possible. Indeed, it might have been acceptable to start with for a God to claim everything, but everything covers a lot of ground and everyone needs someone to help with the paperwork, so to speak.

Therefore, these under-Gods and sub-Goddesses needed to spread out. They claimed their own departments, operating budgets and bylaws. Becoming, like so many institutions, indispensable and totally without merit. But it didn't stop there. What of the next generation of little Gods and Godlings? Well, when things were younger it wasn't so bad - Thor could inherit the hammer and Pantheon from Odin with next to no qualifications and little talk of nepotism as it was still a family business.

But with more people comes more need of Godding, and not just local Godding, we're talking big, publicly listed multi-national Godhood now. While you still have the big Gods, with their qualifications in Thunder and Buggery from large, well known Universities; for each one of these there are dozens of Godlings who have to make do with the equivalent of Bognor Regis College of Art and Humanities for their education, and you will find them on the fringes of Godly society, living in their parents' underworlds and doing odd jobs and agency work here and there.

You can imagine overhearing a conversation at the Celestial job centre such as "we need holiday cover for the wettest six weeks of the 'summer' for caravan parks in North Wales. Shall I put your name forwards?" – careers are born from this. Or alternatively, many of the more determined new Gods are now starting to become self-employed. For every God that makes people congregate in their church, chapel, or temple in any form; there are plenty more just lurking around scraping for any shred of belief they can cling on to.

So, the next time you are putting up a shelf and inexplicably not only find the correct Rawlplugs and the correct sized drill bit on the first go, or roll into a petrol station as your car sips its last dregs of juice - be careful what God you offer praises to as you might just have started a new religion.

And while it has been a pleasure to participate in the genesis of this project, like so many of you have, from the side-lines; it is purely Hannah's imagination, drive and humour which have brought so many of these deity-like creations from obscurity out into the world; and while this book must surely count as religious material (especially for tax purposes), the altars newly discovered, yet fully traditional, are your own. I trust many of you will be joining me in worship soon.

Dr Gareth Wilden 2019

PATELLA

Goddess of Dodgy Knees

Some philosophers say that faith is a crutch, but the philosophy of the followers of Patella is to put their faith in a crutch. Patella has numerous Temples around the world, including ones in; Stepney (UK), Krzywe Kolanois (Poland), and Stiffknee Knob (NC - USA).

There are no stairs in Patella's temples. Every comfortable pew is accompanied by its own soft pouffé for the elevation of aching limbs. Hot and cold compress hassocks are available to borrow for a small donation. All prayers are offered from a seated position. Repeated standing and kneeling for prayer is not required. Patella understands.

Patella's Sabbath day is Saturday. The rites of Patella can induce a euphoria in her worshippers which makes them weak at the knees, known as "Saturday Night Femur". Other faiths experience "the rapture", followers of Patella experience "the rupture". During services "Groaning Hymns" are sung by her choirs, accompanied by trom-bones, in perfect harmon-knee. (One of the most famous of her sacred works is Mike Oldfield's "Tubular Bandages".) A sacrament of rubbing alcohol and Ibuprofen is shared by the congregation during the service. You are advised to partake sparingly, or you may get inkneebriated. At the close of a ritual, instead of applause, the gathered faithful will crack their joints as they rise to make a clickophony of appreciation.

They are a very benevolent religion. The faithful will always hop to it if they see an opportunity to help the kneedy. They often co-ordinate multi agency disaster relief aid, as they are really good at managing a joint effort. In addition they are big believers in justice and fairness and her church provides free legal representation to accused persons who cannot afford a legal counsel. Especially those hopeless cases who don't have a leg to stand on. Beneficiaries will confirm that they are highly skilled barristers, and have often described them as "the bee's knees".

Her clergy can be identified by their distinctive official headwear known as the "Knee Cap". In countries where religions are suppressed and they must act in secret, her followers will identify themselves to one another via the secret "Limp Handshake". The mystics of Patella, are said to be able to predict the weather via their aching joints. When a new member is inducted into the priesthood they are ceremonially anointed with Deep Heat.

Patella was Christianised as the Cornish Pre-congregation saints, the twin sisters St Fibula and St Tibia. In the Ancient Greek pantheon her equivalent is the deity Dodgyknees. ✳

(If you find the puns in this one too painful, just try to appreciate the iron knee.) .

QUINOA

God of Faddy Diets

If you thought the rules of Halal, Kashrut or the Bhagavad Gita were hard to follow, you haven't tried following the way of Quinoa. He is an underground deity who goes against the grain. In the story of his origin, he was an Aztec mortal man who drowned in the Mainstream but was resurrected and elevated to god-hood by...
...well, you've probably never heard of him.

The first person to follow the way of Quinoa did it, "About, like 100 years before anyone else did, man". The rest say they are doing it ironically. Followers of Quinoa always have burnt tongues because they ate food before it was cool. They can be distinguished by their excessively product laden, obsessively groomed facial hair, heavy framed glasses with plain glass in them and red trousers. They often ride to the temple on Penny-farthing bicycles.

There are regular rites held in Quinoa's temples. These are mainly long winded lectures on artisanal food production based on tenuous science. The cult of Quinoa encourages the use of microwaves. They don't like conventional ovens. The section of the service that would be called the "sermon" in other churches, is known as the "Quinoa-Oat" address. There are occasionally live performances of sacred music on sackbut, glockenspiel and didgeridoo. On especially sacred occasions, they traditionally sing the haunting choral masterpiece Ave Cado. However, more often, music is provided from recordings on VINYL, ALWAYS VINYL!

Quinoa’s temples can be recognised by the jaunty blackboard that stands outside each one. On these a witty and inspirational quote for the day is inscribed. These boards uplift everyone who sees them, and bring all those who miss them crashing down. At Quinoa's temple one can purchase a cup of refreshing coffee that is made from locally sourced ingredients and is free from dairy, sugar, coffee and the dreaded dihydrogen monoxide. Though, it does come with vegan, organic sprinkles. When you hear how much it costs, you'll say " 'kin wha' ?!"

CANNULA

Goddess of Blood Donors

C annula is the goddess of blood donors, anaesthetists and rehydration therapy. In mythology she was the consort of the God Apheresis until they were separated. Sadly, their love was in vein.

Whilst there are a few permanent temples to Cannula, most of her places of worship are temporary pop up affairs. They will often set up in schools, village halls and community centres. There are even a few mobile "Bus Temples" touring the country. The temples of Cannula have a distinctive "green couch and screen" theme to the décor. Inside, the faithful will exchange donations of blood for a cuppa and a fig roll. As they enter the temple, worshippers will deposit a small drop of blood in a mysterious measuring cylinder. This test ascertains whether they will act with the level of specific gravity required whilst inside. If you are found to have "blod" in your veins, then it is because you are typo. Offerings of tea and biscuits are left at her temple by grateful benefactors to supply the donors.

Services of worship often continue all day with visitors coming and going, very much "going with the flow". A typical call and response chant from one of Cannula's rites goes,

Priest 1: Oh! Negative!
Priest 2: Oh! Positive
Priest 1: Hey, negative!
Priest 2: Hey, positive!
Priest 1: Be negative!
Priest 2: Be positive!
Congregation: Hey, be positive!

Following this there will usually be a short resus.

The clergy of Cannula wear pale blue cotton trousers and shirts with upside-down watches pinned to them. They live communally, but will each have a small cell to themselves. Most will live within a small "red cell". However, the most senior clergy have a larger "white cell" in recognition for their role guarding the faith. Her acolytes, priests and priestesses display their rank within the order by wearing small heart shaped badges of bronze, silver or gold. The high priestess drinks only from a cut crystal decanter and tumbler set. ✄

CANDIDA

Goddess of Itchy Privates & Plain Speaking

C andida is a goddess with a very pale complexion and a constant expression of torment. If you are visited by Candida, unlike other deities, she will deliver her directions in no uncertain terms. She can sometimes be a little rash. You won't get vague portents or metaphors from this goddess!

In her mythology she is said to originally have been simply the Goddess of Blunt Truths. She was laid low by an attack from the furious demon Bacterium (because the truth hurts). She was saved by the Goddess Penicillina, but was left with a sense of constant irritation and a pH imbalance.

Her principal temple is located near Scratchy Bottom on the South Coast. Possibly due to the proximity to the sea, there is a distinct piscine aroma to the place.

Her clergy move around the compound using the ceremonial walk, short steps with knees held together and fingers clenched. Any priest or priestess caught walking normally will be given a dishonourable discharge.

Throughout her services her devotees will sit on their hands with their legs crossed as they listen to a forthright sermon.

The temple houses a particularly ornate mighty organ, which is decorated with an intricate relief depicting cavorting crabs. It is played at every service and the congregation must loudly applaud.

The organist tends to get upset if they don't get the clap every week. For some reason, flambéed petit pois (or burning peas) are usually served at temple meals. One should never attempt to steal peas from a priestess's plate. Those are herpeas. Yogurt is also regularly served. Just not at meal times.

Candida is also known as "Throssel", "The Beast from the Yeast" and "Lady Chalk of Billingsgate". She was assimilated by the early Celtic church and Christianised as Saint Albicans. Thrushes are her sacred animals. ✄

WERENTMEE

God of Denial

With the innocent face of an angel, the God Werentmee is impervious to all blame. Any excrement thrown his way slides right off. The divine light shining from his reverent rectum means that any shade thrown does not fall upon him. He has two other avatars not shown here. One is a lyre playing musician with flaming underwear and a nose as long as a telephone wire, and the other is the invisible divine ghost known to children and cyclopes everywhere as "Mr Nobody". Werentmee, God of Denial should not be confused with any Ancient Egyptian river deities. Werentmee hasn't had any dealings in that region since the "The Aswan Dam Wasn't an Environmental Disaster" incident.

The philosophy of the cult of Werentmee is not to avoid the sin, but to avoid the shame and the consequences. His devotees include corrupt politicians, environment destroyers and asset stripping CEOs who sink their companies. Essential personal qualities for joining the priesthood of Werentmee are twinkling charm, a posh accent, and a very short memory. Having a conscience is considered to be a severe handicap, and may render one unsuitable to serve. Werentmee's priests can be recognised by the distinctive mittens they wear to prevent any finger-pointing. They always wear spotless whiter than white robes. The priesthood always tackle every task or project in a team of at least 6. This is "herd action" a defensive precaution. A team structure makes it nigh on impossible to isolate any single under-performing individual. The High Priest of Werentmee is known by the title "Pastor Buck". He travels constantly in the pursuit of his duties, serving the faith tirelessly. "The Buck" never, ever stops. He is aided in his work by the Treasurer, Mr Scott Free and the Secretary, Patsy.

The roof of the Temple of Werentmee bristles with cruel spikes, scarecrows and decoy birds of prey. Atop all this sits a priest in the highest room of the tallest tower with a shot gun. Anything to prevent the pigeons from coming home to roost. The interior of his temple is strangely decorated to appear as though it is a photographic negative. Black is white in there. The Temple also houses the sacred animals. At the centre of the menagerie is a large lake, in which live a bask of Crocodylus lacrimosa (a kind of salt water crocodile). In the field around the lake graze a flock of the rare goat breed Capra piaculum (or Scapegoat). The temple has innumerable entrances. When you visit, will you enter via the Watergate, the Hackgate, the Toddlergate or the Camillagate? Last year an attempt to film a special episode of Masterchef in the Temple of Werentmee was abandoned because the butter wouldn't melt.

Many seek the divine assistance of Werentmee to get themselves out of a spot of bother of their own making. For serious misdemeanours they will attend the temple and take part in a rite where one of the Scapegoats is sacrificed and burned on a pyre of shredded documents and compromising photographs. For less serious quotidian situations, the temple press publishes a handy reference list of societal groups that you can blame for your daily fails. For example, today's list includes: young people, teachers, parents, snowflakes, liberal lefties, immigrants, the European Union, women, and the weather. Werentmee is often mentioned in the mythology of other faiths. Usually as a filthy piece of toe rag with a cherubic face who will ultimately bring about the end of days. ✄

FLATULA

Goddess of Girl Farts

Not the most popular deity, and rarely worshiped in confined spaces. The ethos of Flatula is "Wherever you be, let your wind blow free". She is considered uncouth by approximately 50% of people, the rest find her hilarious. The Flatula mythology contains a devil figure called "Yakult" who continually seeks to destroy Flatula's divine wind. Her consort is "Throu" God of Digestion. It is generally considered to be better to follow Flatula than to follow Throu.

Followers of Flatula traditionally greet each other with their index finger outstretched and the words "Digitus meus trahere". They adhere to a strict diet of only beans, mushy peas, cauliflower and eggs in order to ensure a constant production of pious maft. Her acolytes are, without exception, proud of their faith and evangelise enthusiastically. They never ever deny it, they always supply it.

The vestments of her clergy are designed to lift and waft humorously at the slightest zephyr. At their initiation into the priesthood they will be given a tattoo of a stylised gust of wind on their arms. This is known as "wearing your fart on your sleeve". In their spare time the priesthood like to play a board game using bronze playing cards. One cannot buy the bronze playing cards for this game from shops. They have to make them themselves. So a player will have had to smelt it before they dealt it. The priestesses of Flatula are renowned as skilled physicians. Should you consult them, they will perform a thorough diagnosis which will include taking your fart rate.

The temples of Flatua have elegant, sculpted frontage supported by shapely columns, topped by two twin domes with a chimney between them. There are many unglazed windows to ensure adequate ventilation. Inside the walls are decorated with aesthetic airbrushed murals. These are created by the artist blowing droplets of paint onto the wall using their bottom breath. This distinctive style is known as Pop Fart Art. There is no limit to the time one may remain in her temple and admire the paintings and the aromas. If you can't get enough of that wonderful guff, you can stay to your fart's content.

The temple musicians play throughout the day in her honour. Her best known pieces of sacred music include "Fanfare for the Common Woman", "There Goes the Elephant" and "Shoot that Duck". The only instruments permitted to be played in her temple are the Kazoo, the rattle and the sackbutt.

Flatula is closely associated with the Viking Goddess Queef. She has many variants in pantheons across the world, she seems to be a deity who resonates with many people. Ironically, should Flatula appear to you, you should not break wind before her. It's her turn. ✄

HÆMORRHOID

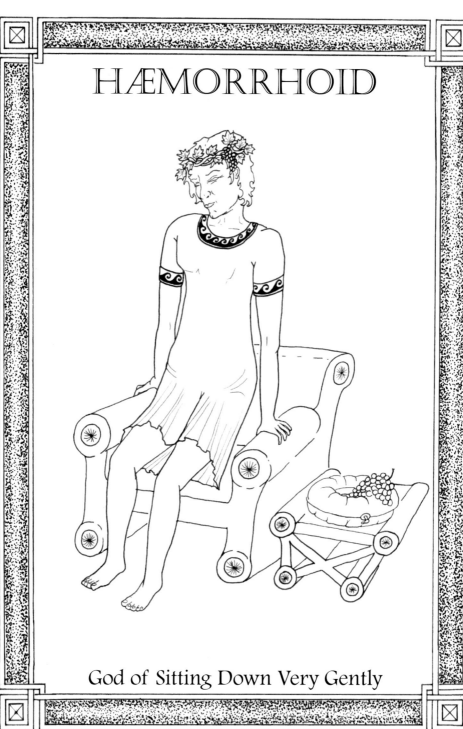

God of Sitting Down Very Gently

Haemorrhoid is a god of the nether world and of things you can't kiss better. No one is sure what he stands for, but he stands none the less. He was cursed to never, ever sit down comfortably again by one of the winter goddesses for daring to sit on her cold stone throne. Haemorrhoid is said to have two sacred animals. One is a mythical giant lizard known as the Megasaurarse, and an obstreperous donkey who is a real pain in the ass.

If you attend a ritual, you will find that the standing areas of the temple fill up first. Arrive too late and you'll find it's sitting room only. When the priest in the Temple of Haemorrhoid says "Let us be seated" to the congregation, what follows is a drawn out ballet of gentle pliés to the accompaniment of a chorus of muted groans. This is despite the fact that every pew is generously cushioned. At the end of every service the congregation leap to their feet and give the priest a standing ovation. Up on the high altar a small bunch of sacred grapes rests on an inflatable donut-shaped cushion. In fact the decor of the entire temple has a "grapey" theme.

Haemorrhoid is worshipped by almost everyone at some point in their lives, with the exception of perfect arseholes. Giles is the most popular given name for Haemorrhoidian boys, and they often grow up to become farmers. Emma is the most popular girls name. Infants are inducted into the faith by being baptised in the "Chalfont".

Astrology is very important to Haemorrhoidians. Their predictions and calendar are based around the movements of Uranus. It is considered to be the most significant of the planets to observe because Uranus is so large and gassy. They watch the skies especially carefully for the significant and rare phenomena when a mysterious red streak appears in the sky near the planet. This event is known as Uranus Bleeding. Their astrologers and seers have predicted that the world will eventually end with a giant assteroid impact.

You are advised never to provoke a priest or priestess of Haemorrhoid. The constant standing, itching and general discomfort turns them into very short tempered bad asses. They have been known to fly into states of red misted fury known as a "Haemorrhoid Rage".

You may be surprised to learn that the priestesses of Haemorrhoid run a chain of "Gentleman's Clubs", the proceeds of which support their church. Here, for a generous tip, they will perform an unusual form of erotic entertainment known as the Pro Laps Dance.

Worshippers of Haemorrhoid gather annually at the summer solstice. On this occasion a specially brewed beer called a Pilesner is consumed. At the climax of the ceremony the priests stand together to watch the sun rise and greet the red eye of the dawn with the cry "Arise Oh Anusol!" ✳

GANACHE

God of Chocolate, Cream Cakes and
Words that Sound Rude but aren't.

anache is a kindly deity who watches over bakers and confectioners. He may have a rotund figure, but he still has amazing buns. Offering a prayer to Ganache as you add the cocoa to your cake recipe is said to prevent soggy bottoms, provided you also give the batter a good ritual forking. He is the remover of bits of stray egg shell.

Delicious cooking smells waft from his temple, luring in new devotees. Every year at his festival, the priests make a giant cream horn (said to represent his tusk) which is shared amongst his followers as a fertility rite. Followers of Ganache define a "balanced diet" as a cupcake in each hand.

Ganache has a mischievous side and a prehensile trunk for snatching delicious treats. When a Ganachite baker places 12 cakes on the cooling rack and returns to find only 11, instead of shouting at his apprentices he will shrug and say, "I see Ganache has taken his own offering." It is considered a divine endorsement of your skill and a blessing if Ganache just could not resist.

Ganache is also the God of words that sound a bit rude, but actually aren't. Like "masticate" and "kumquat".

Ganache is said to be quite an emotionally sensitive deity. When something goes wrong, he takes a while to gateauxverit. He is often in tiers.

Followers of Ganache believe that you only get out of life what you pudding. They also value the pursuit of independence, it is frowned upon to sponge off anyone. Ganache is an extremely popular deity and is worshipped by hundreds and thousands.

If you believe in Ganache you are encouraged to d'éclair it loudly and proudly. ✂

PHILTRUM

God of Things Right Under Your Nose

Normally Philtrum is associated with Monday mornings, but he also does post bank holiday Tuesdays. He is especially worshipped by persons over the age of forty and stressed people. Philtrum specialises in keys, pens, phones and anything you just put down a moment ago. He also does glasses on foreheads. One time when he couldn't find his laurels, it was because he was resting on them.

Temples of Philtrum are designed on a theme of "Lost Halves of Pairs". The floor is carpeted with a quilt of odd socks, and the curtains are made from a textile collage of lost gloves. It is illuminated by chandeliers made from single earrings and cufflinks. There are many comfortable sofas upholstered with a fabric woven from shoelaces and phone charger cables. The defences around the temple are fortified against infidels by having thousands of lost, single knitting needles set into the top of the wall pointing skywards.

The correct procedure for visiting a Temple of Philtrum is to walk in, stare blankly into space for a moment, meditate upon what it was you went in for, and then leave again quietly with the minimum possible embarrassment. If you do decide to stay awhile, take a seat on one of the comfy sofas and contemplate what you are searching for. Then try reaching down the back of said sofa. Seek and ye may find if Philtrum sees fit to answer your prayers.

The priests of Philtrum are known as "Searchers". They aspire to achieve vagueness in all things. The philosophy being that if you don't know where anything is anyway, do you ever really, truly lose something? This only applies to the personal life of a devoted acolyte though. The priests also serve to help the lay congregation find what they have mislaid.

The sacred Book of Philtrum is called "The Libro de Claris". The original copy has not been seen in years. They think they may have lent it to someone. The following is a short extract from the text:

Perdue, a man of the town, cried in his torment, "Oh mighty Philtrum! Have you seen my wallet? I know I had it only a moment ago." And Philtrum replied, "Well, where did you last have it?" Perdue said, "I put it down on the kitchen table, oh Lord, but it isn't there now." In his wisdom Philtrum spake, "Have you tried looking in the fridge?" Perdue looked in the fridge, and by a divine miracle against all the physical laws of the universe, lo there was his wallet by the sausages. He cried, "Praise be to Philtrum! For now I shall be on time for my date and I am on a promise."

Followers of Philtrum indicate their membership of the faith by carrying extra large ceremonial handkerchiefs... ...which they can never find when they need them. . ✂

CHARDONNAY

Goddess of Awkward Work Socials & Barbecues

Shortly after the concept of employment began, way back in human prehistory, the excruciating torture of the work social evolved. In answer to a million desperate glances at watches, Chardonnay rose fully formed from the ashes of a barbeque to watch over all those hiding in the shrubbery and sobbing into their fourth cocktail. Chardonnay is always dressed smart-casual but is constantly desperate to take off her bra and slip into her pyjamas.

Worship of Chardonnay tends to take place in hired venues or outdoors. Any service you attend will somehow always also be attended by the same people you've had to put up with all week. The rites typically commence with lighting a ritual charcoal fire an hour in advance and then burning some sacrificial sausages on it. There will then usually be either a pre ordered set meal (where no one can remember what they chose to eat 2 months ago), or a dry and curly buffet where some Heston Blumenfool has mixed up the vegetarian and meaty sandwiches for "presentation" reasons. Following this disappointing repast there will be a lengthy address by the High Priest or "Boss" which will try desperately to be funny, and fail.

Throughout, wine and ale will flow freely and worshippers must attempt to consume enough to lubricate their tolerance for the rest of the congregation whilst avoiding vomiting, crying or paralysis. The service will conclude with a sacred dance, usually to music from about 10 years ago. No one knows the correct moves to this dance, so they just stand in cliquey circles and jig on the spot awkwardly.

At special festivals, worshippers will draw lots to make a small, anonymous gift to a fellow worshipper that they could not give the tiny furry crack of a dead rat's behind about. As the faithful have a tendency to gift each other bootleg recordings of Latin influenced psychedelic rock music, this tradition has become known as the Secret Santana. There are a few permanent Temples of Chardonnay. Their interiors are decorated with thousands of photocopies of bare bottoms. As you leave the Temple of Chardonnay a drunken wasp will be waiting to challenge you to a fight.

There are a few strange people out there who are genuinely enthusiastic followers of Chardonnay. Most people attending her rites are merely doing so out of a sense of duty, in an attempt at career advancement or to try and get "better acquainted" with Mo from accounts. These endeavours rarely end well. ✄

LATRINE

Goddess of Music Festivals

Latrine is principally a summer Goddess. Many think she originated in the 1960s, but in fact she is much, much older. It is said she was formed from the mud churned by the feet and spilled beer of the first humans to gather and entertain each other with turns around the campfire. She has no permanent temple, all music festivals are her sacred spaces. Latrine has the power to maintain good spirits in any weather. No matter how much it rains, she's never a stick in the mud.

Attending a ritual of worship for Latrine can be a full on and taxing (at 20%), though worthwhile experience. Whilst there are many small and family friendly services around the country every year, the most famous are bewilderingly huge. She is such a widely loved deity that, in order to attend the most popular gatherings, one must first engage in either a multi million pound auction, have a top notch internet connection and the fastest "refresh key finger" in the west or be prepared to throw-down in a vegan street-fight. Following this one must muster one's survival equipment and journey to try and find a patch of field big enough for your tent within a mile walk of the main stage.

There is a photograph of the crowd watching R.E.M. play "Losing My Religion" at Glastonbury 1999 which is said to have captured an apparition of Latrine. If you look carefully, that's her in the corner. She seems to be divinely illuminated by a heavenly spotlight. Latrine has been known to work miracles for the musicians, performers and crew who strive to stage her rites. One legendary tale, told in revered tones in green rooms around the world, is of how she came to the rescue of The Who. Their minibus ran out of petrol on the way to the Reading Festival in 1966 on a remote country road where they could see for miles and miles with no sign of civilization. The band were just thinking "We won't get fuelled again!" when Latrine appeared to them with a full fuel can. They asked "Who are you?" but she just smiled and kept her secrets behind blue eyes. Henceforth this blessed vehicle has become known as The Magic Bus.

The most holy sanctuary within the festival site is the Port-a-Loo. Visiting one is an essential necessity of the proper order of worship. Inside one will receive enlightenment into the full spectrum of the human condition. If Latrine is smiling upon you, your visit will be timed just after her angels in biohazard suits with the sludge-gulper have refreshed the cubicle. For the 0.0956 nanoseconds following their visit, there will be toilet paper and a slightly less pungent odour.

The priests and priestesses of Latrine can be identified by their "Crew" wristbands and AAA laminates. Each festival their role begins as one of organisation, transitions into damage limitation, and ends as a disaster area clean up operation. Worshippers who leave a mess are not considered to be the true faithful by the inner circle. Blessed are those who use a bin. Some clergy are trained specifically as healers to man the first aid tent. They are said to be highly skilled medics as they know the difference between Placebo and The Cure. The security priests have health and safety as their paramount concern. This is why they insist that everybody looks at their hands whilst dancing. Latrine's greatest powers are her ability to open your mind to new experiences, to create happy memories and the feeling that it was all worth it. She is also known to the Romans as "Domum Stercore". ✄

WANTOO

God of Sound Engineers

Wantoo is the sound engineer of the Gods. He sits amongst the mass of mortals and controls the volume and quality of the music of the spheres. He is the master of the gate to heavenly music. Legends tell of the origin of his golden mixing desk, which was touched by King Midas. Safe in Wantoo's capable hands, the other deities can speakon with confidence that they will be clearly heard. Wantoo is assisted by his faithful roadie Jack Plug, who does the heavy lifting and his consort Lampie, the Goddess of Heavenly Lighting. The sacred text of Wantoo is called "The Spirit Folio".

Wantoo is always depicted wearing a distinctive net skirt, known as the Wantoo Tutu, which is also worn by his priesthood. Wantoo's priests learn to master the art of sound engineering to try to achieve divine perfect sound for lesser mortal musicians. Despite this noble intent, the relationship between Wantoo and musicians is sometimes strained. They say that the difference between a Priest of Wantoo and a toilet is that a toilet only has to take crap from one arsehole at once. Divas should beware though. Wantoo watches over his priests and if provoked too far he will use "Strongbow" his mighty weapon of divine smiting. He often uses Strongbow to reduce musicians with egos to pillars of salt.

The Commandments of Wantoo
- Thou shalt change thy battery before each gig.
- Thou shalt bring thine own instrument cable and a spare.
- Thou shalt learn what all thy knobs and pedals do.
- Thou shalt wrap cables properly.
- Thou shalt not use thine own vocal effects.
- Thou shalt play thy drum kit appropriately for the room.
- Thou shalt not keep asking to be turned up in the monitors.
- Though shalt have a tuner and use it.
- Thou shalt drink only from the sports-cap bottle whilst onstage.
- Thou shalt not play whilst other artists are sound checking.
- Thou shalt not over run thy set time.

Those who break these commandments will be banished to back beyond the monitor desk.

Temples of Wantoo are often found in pub back rooms and cellar venues. The floor inside is printed with the traditional "sticky glaze" to encourage visitors to stay as long as possible. Worshippers will try to cluster as close as possible to the altar, situated in the centre-rear of the knave, to experience the best sound. A typical service will comprise a two hour sound check and a half hour of homily. Worship always ends with a call and response between the priest and congregation such as,

Priest: Go in peace. We gather again next Wednesday.
Congregation: Yes, it is very windy.
Priest: Wendy will be holding a bake sale on Thursday.
Congregation: Me too, let's go for a pint.

Wantoo also appears in the Roman pantheon as Tinnatus and was Christianised as St Alan du Heath. . ✖

FUTON

God of Temporary Sleeping Arrangements

Futon is the saviour of: gap year students, couch surfers, disgraced spouses, musicians on tour, inebriated post-party people, and guys who said something stupid and blew their chances after being invited in for coffee and the departure of the last bus. Known in other regions as Zed, Camp or Murphy, he is also the God of Poor Compromises.

Futon is a deity who has wandered and explored the whole world with his jazz dot and djembe in search of himself. (Unless you have about three days to spare DO NOT ask him about it). He has both penetrated and absorbed aspects of many different cultures since his origin in Japan. His appearance has become heavily westernised as his popularity has spread. He originally had two avatars "Shikifuton" and "Kakefuton".

The way of Futon is a very fatalistic philosophy. They believe that; nothing really mattress, the way to achieve inner peace is to chair less and that flexibility in an uncertain world is key to being bedder than all the rest.

Futon's temple is renowned for providing accommodation for the stranded and the needy day or night. If you attend a ritual or rite of worship at Futon's temple you will be initially impressed at the seating provided for worshippers with it's downy padding. However, this will somehow, magically become less and less pleasant over time. Unless you are under 25, you will leave the temple half crippled. In fact, if you are under 25 you will probably think Futon is pretty (sic.) sick, if you are over 25 you will probably find him to be a bit of a pretentious twat who makes you uncomfortable.

I strongly advise you not to heed the family planning guidance issued by Futon's sect. It has been found to be woefully inaccurate. It is, in fact, still possible to get pregnant on a pull-out bed. (Although, Futon does have the power to make lovers disappear, and so may be effective in that way.)

Despite the curse on the love lives of his followers, Futon does have a divine consort himself. His wife Vango is a minor goddess of sleep and dreams. In his grumpier moments Futon has been heard to unkindly refer to her as "The Sleeping Bag". This is grossly unfair to this fluffy, warm and protective deity. Due to partly mortal heritage, Vango spends only 9 month of the year as a goddess, and 3 as a mortal. She is a three season goddess.

There is a variation of Yoga associated with the worship of Futon. It only has two asanas "Sit" and "Lay". ✄

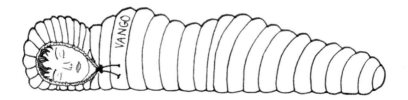

DAVE

God of Perfect Mates

D ave is a legend and top quality banter merchant. He is a deity who will always stand his round. He is the god you can call on at 3am. The god who you know would help you with anything from moving house to hiding the bodies. Dave works in IT and he WILL fix your laptop.

In his mythology Dave is the wing man of the gods. Happily married to "Beckki - Goddess of BFFs", Dave will happily introduce his single friends to the disappointed deities who approach him. He can also be persuaded to remove his shirt on hot days in the Olympic Park to entice passing gaggles of goddesses into striking up an idle conversation.

Followers will greet each other warmly with bone-crushing hugs, where the groins remain a respectable distance apart, and the words "How are you, you old bastard!".

What happens in the Temple of Dave stays in the Temple of Dave. When a true devotee of Dave enters his temple, their wi-fi connects automatically. The temple has many attractions including; a superb collection of vintage and modern games consoles, a big-screen TV (Dave gets all the sports and movie channels), a pool table, a barista machine (Dave is Italian by descent) and a dartboard. There are no hard wooden pews in Dave's temple. It's reclining massage chairs for all!

The grounds of the temple house a comprehensively equipped workshop where Dave's priests will happily help a devotee fix their bike, car or lawnmower. Next to this is a soundproof band rehearsal and recording studio with a collection of vintage guitars for impromptu jam sessions. There is also a basketball hoop and enough lawn for a kick about, with a couple of jumpers on the ground to mark the goalposts. The congregation are always shirts and the priesthood are skins. On visiting his temple, you may be asked to donate a tenner. Don't worry. Dave will always pay you back.

The priests of Dave are renowned for being larger than life and excellent home-brewers. During communion with Dave the beer flows freely and worshippers consume this with "Friend Chips". You can even take a six-pack of "Dave" away with you. If you imbibe, the priests will let you sleep over or see you safely home. Dave does not let his followers drive drunk.

Sadly, Dave has been barred from "The Virgin's Arms" over a bit of a disagreement over the tab. His sacred animal is a slightly wiffy mongrel dog that cadges crisps by doing tricks. ✄

(Inspiration for Dave came entirely from Michelangelo di Lodovico Buonarroti Simoni. Cheers Mick! Yer a true mate! .)

ERIC

God of Pub Games

Eric, the God of Pub Games is an extremely Ancient Deity. He is known to predate the founding of the Olympic Games in 776 BCE. He was the patron deity of the earlier and now forgotten Olympub Games. The date that the Olympub games were founded is now lost to antiquity, but they may have begun the first time Neolithic humans gathered and competed to throw a loop of string over a stick whilst consuming dangerous quantities of proto-ale. The religion then spread rapidly, and the first temple to Eric was built as a simple circle of tall rectangular standing stones, stood on their ends. This design was soon copied many times across the ancient world in what seems to have been a kind of domino effect.

The worship of Eric centres around developing the mind, body and character through the playing of social games of skill and chance. These are also believed to bond communities, families and friends together through communal worship. Some detractors say that the religion of Eric is a load of bulls hit, but his faithful will tell you he's okey.

Eric's modern places of worship are less like temples and more like saloons. The main structure is traditionally in the shape of two large adjoined circus tents, a structure known as a "double top". The interior décor trends heavily towards dark green leather, baize and wood panelling. It is divided into 9 different chapels, each dedicated to one of the 9 Sacred Sports; darts, pool, billiards, poker, cribbage, skittles, dice, ring toss and shove ha'penny. His temples often have quirky colloquial names such as "The Ham and Cheese", "The Shuffle and Board" and "The Curly Cue". Every temple has a small crowd of bored children sat outside on some broken swings. Each one forlornly clutches a bottle of Vimto with a straw and a bag of crisps.

The Chapel of Darts is a risky and unnerving place to enter. In fact it's so scary that some people immediately do a 180 and leave. Some worshippers are there to try and overcome their "Projectile Dysfunction", so be ready to duck. (Treatment for this condition can be expensive, so most only resort to it when they are in the throws of despair.) The Chapel of Darts also contains a confessional where one can gain spiritual solace and atonement by divulging ones darty secrets. If you are travelling to visit the Chapel of Darts, it is best to avoid cheap flights.

The Chapel of Pool is perhaps the tensest place in the temple. Here worshippers stare one another out to see who will break first. The corridor to the chapel has a lengthy line of 50p's laid along its length. Anyone arriving and arbitrarily deciding that "winner stays on" will be forced to eat 50 cubes of blue chalk. The Chapel of Pool is particularly popular with younger members of the faith. They often study there in hopes of being professional pool players when they grow up. Until they realise they can't have it both ways. Worshippers are welcome to stay all day, but are asked to pop outside if they need to pot a brown or get the urge to sink the pink.

The Priests and Priestesses of Eric organise and arbitrate all the games within the temple. The High Priestess is renowned for her stern and unemotional visage when passing judgement. However much you are tempted, you are advised not to poke her face to see if it's real.

GARNISH

God of Superfluous Vegetables

Garnish is a purely decorative deity. He is particularly associated with any fruit or vegetable one would never normally eat on its own, such as parsley, lemons and radishes carved into the shape of roses. He crops up in slight variations in many pantheons, but is thought to have originally been a Romaine God.

In all traditions his consort is the Goddess Dirti Martini. She is a little salty. However, Garnish is said to not always be faithful, and to have pursued mortal lovers. You will know if Garnish has amorous intentions towards you as he will send you a dick pickle.

Garnish's temple is instantly recognisable by the paper parasol, pineapple wedge and sparkler sticking out of the chimney. It is always artfully presented and kept in mint condition. Adjacent to the Temple is a cemetery where the distinguished followers of Garnish are berried. Inside the temple, tiny offerings of artfully arranged foodstuffs are placed on the altar daily. During their annual fertility festival, these offerings are designed to resemble genitalia. This special kind of votive is known as an "Amuse Bush". They joke that one should never eat an offering to Garnish oneself, and it may be that many a true word spoken is ingest. Or maybe Garnish actually doesn't grately carrot all.

Followers of Garnish will acknowledge one another with the greeting "Olive you!". Every rite in his temple begins with the line, "Lettuce pray". A common meditative aid used by followers of Garnish is to draw intricate Mandalas on oversized white plates using "jus" or "coulis".

The current High Priest is called Elvis Parsley, his consort Rosemary serves as High Priestess. Together they are responsible for spreading good chives and delivering sage advice. They always make thyme for their congregation and love grows where Rosemary goes. Sadly, despite serving him with relish, all the clergy of Garnish have their wages deducted slightly each month.

One specialist sect of Garnish's priesthood are researchers in Molecular Biology. They have succeeded in engineering several new species. The most popular of these may be the "Pimento Olive". The genes of a pepper were spliced into a green olive tree so that a tiny piquant pepper grows inside each olive in place of the stone.

The first commandment of Garnish is: Avacadon't. ✄

PICCÆOLUS

God of Flautists & Wind Musicians

Piccaeolus is a musical deity with equivalent avatars in the pantheons of many cultures. He is also known as Kazooka, Flautulus, Djethro and Flautingale. He watches over all wind musicians, particularly players of the Pink Piccolo. The story of his origin states that he was a mortal war child (yes, he was living, in the past) from Rock Island. He shot to fame with his musical performance in a Passion Play. Whilst out one night on storm watch, he was wearing the crest of a knave and a broadsword. This attracted a lightning strike which scorched him and the tree he was stood under from roots to branches. He was resurrected by a remorseful thunder god and elevated to the godhood to serve as minstrel to the gods. Initially the thunder god wanted to keep this under wraps, but Piccaeolus couldn't wait to stand up and was soon bursting out.

The Temple of Piccaeolus is located in Galway. It is a tall, narrow, cylindrical stone tower with nine ovoid windows. It is carved from silvery Andersonite and features elegant fluted columns. It, perhaps sensibly, does not have any glass in the windows. At all times within the temple there will be two flutes being played by minstrels in the gallery. They play the sacred music of Piccaeolus in unison with a minor second interval. There are no temple cats. Or if there were any, they fled long ago. The temple has never ever been cleaned inside, although the outside is very shiny. Hidden to the rear is a constantly dripping outflow tap from which a clear, slimy substance oozes constantly.

At the Temple flautists can study the art of making Romantic music with the priests. The priesthood are renowned experts in tonging and you will marvel at their fingering technique. You cannot help but improve under their tutelage. They can even teach you the techniques of "Survival Musicianship". For example making emergency flutes carved from gherkins. These makeshift instruments are known as Pickle-os. The sacred text of Piccaeolus "Songs from the Wood" will form the core of your syllabus. Be sure to be attentive and keep up in lessons. You don't want them to think you're as thick as a brick. (Interestingly, Piccaeolus himself is illiterate. He doesn't reed music at all.)

The priests and priestesses of Piccaeolus also often act as trusted, secure couriers of valuable and sensitive items. They place the items in their care into flute cases, as this means they will never, ever get stolen. However, should you attempt to intercept them, beware! They practice a deadly martial art which involves firing darts from transverse blow-pipes whist standing on one leg to confuse the enemy. The priesthood and more devout followers of Piccaeolus can be recognised by the wearing of the traditional prayer or "Soul Stice" bells around the feet. There is a fundamentalist sect who go everywhere riding heavy horses and wearing aqualungs.

The followers of Piccaeolus are renowned for all being a little eccentric. In truth every one's a fruit and nut case. Within the faith of Piccaeolus it is possible to marry one's musical instrument. In fact, many senior priests do this as an act of devotion. This unusual wedding ritual is very beautiful and moving. Guests will often tear up when the High Priest says "I now pronounce you Man and Fife". The faith of Piccaeolus is for life. You are still welcome in their community when you're too old to rock and roll. ✾

GLANDULA

Goddess of Electrical Connections

A highly charged and energetic deity with a short fuse who generates a huge following. Glandula's temple is a well insulated building, securely bonded to the earth. The grounds are planted with lovingly grown power plants. Three bronze towers rise above the roof (one slightly taller than the other two).

Following the way of Glandula will certainly change your life. She is something of a transformer and will help keep your spirit level. A key aspect of spiritual development is believed to be the mastering of certain physical exercises. These include Ladder Balancing, the SWArpent Dance and daily acrobatic volting. These exercises are accompanied by meditations on the question "Watt is Love". Persons who severely err in following the way of Glandula sometimes punish themselves using a CAT5 O'Nine Tails until they are P.O.E. faced.

Sight-seers visiting the temple must have 10p for the meter to enter. On certain holy days they lose this charge and the tourists are ex-static. It surprises most visitors to discover that her temple contains a drinking establishment known as "The Buzz Bar". In the bar there are strippers and one can get a really good screwdriver. Sometimes there is even a three way.

It is a long road of practice, training and study spanning several years to become a priest or priestess of Glandula, also known as a "Sparkie". Trainees will live at the temple, which becomes an ohm from home. In training they will pass through three phases. Phluorescentlytes (the starters), Incandescentlytes and Tracklytes. Tracklytes are the most senior, experienced and broad minded priests. Nothing shocks them anymore.

The Tracklytes then divide further into three "Cores". The "Earth Core" are concerned with moral safety. They wear robes of green and yellow. The "Neutral Core" in their blue robes are mediators and negotiators. The "Live Core" wear brown and are concerned with preaching, teaching and sacred arts performance. The high priestess of Glandula is called Electra. She is a somewhat rotund lady, but she prefers the description "well insulated".

One, slightly unsavoury, tradition of the culture surrounding Glandula's faith is the sport of competitive urination. It is believed to have originated due to terrible welfare provisions on building sites, causing Sparkies to have to get creative in order to relieve themselves. The "aim" of this competition is to neatly land one's stream into the toilet bowl from various locations (or zones). Competitors are ranked by their I Pee rating. An I Pee 64 ranked athlete can direct their golden shower into the porcelain from by the sink (zone 2) and an I Pee 67 can land theirs successfully whilst sitting in the bath (zone 0). The number one cede is ranked at I Pee 69 (don't ask).

Her scripture is regularly revised and updated by the ten most senior priests (known as Glandula's Upper Ten or the GU10). They have just released the 18th Edition of her holy book (it's light blue). This senior priesthood undergo constant moral scrutiny themselves, and have limited terms of office, as it is well known that power corrupts. They have to annually undergo a Priest Assessment Test (or PAT test) to ensure continued integrity and that they are well grounded. ✻

MANDLE

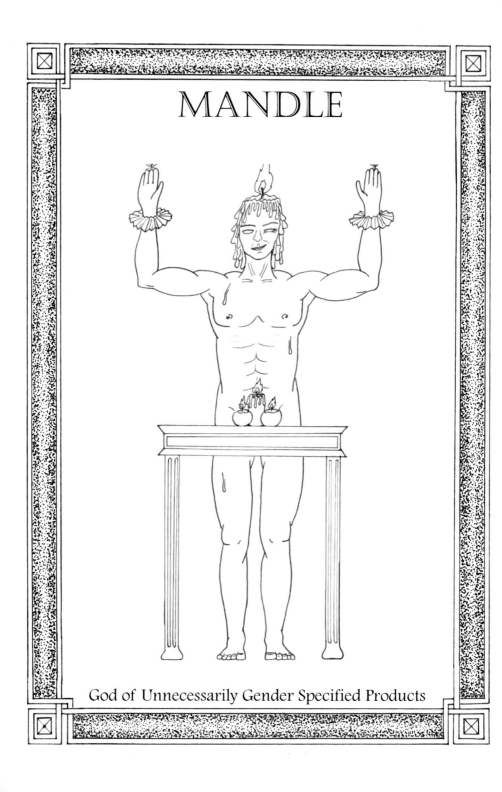

God of Unnecessarily Gender Specified Products

Mandle is the tealightful God of any and all products which are unnecessarily "gender customised" for men. There was once talk that simple products such as soap, pens and candles could be universally designed for all genders. However, such an ideas really get on Mandle's wick. He won' tallow such nonsense.

Following the path of Mandle is said to be spiritually illuminating. An advent-ture for the soul. Although the faith of some may taper off over the years, if you stick with it, you will eventually become enlightened. Actually, their literature says "lit". One hopes this is metaphorical.

Every item in Mandle's temple is specifically formulated "FOR MEN". From the camo pattern sandpaper and porcupine quill toilet roll in the bathroom to the he-lights on the altar. An impressive display of relics and sacred artefacts are lovingly displayed on the Mandlepiece. Perhaps the most revered of these are the Holy Packet of McCoys, the Blessed Yorkiebah and a box of giant tissues.

When visiting the temple, worshippers are encouraged to make a donation, light a small candle and pray to be more self assured. This is called the votive confidence. Whilst visiting, do take the time to try one of their "Bronuts", a deep fried dough delicacy made and sold by the clergy.

His priests are called "Lu-menz" and the high priest is called "The Candelabro". They are flambeauant in their worship, and attending one of their rituals is said to be guaranteed to brighten your day. Given the slightest invitation they will wax lyrical about Mandle for hours.

Followers of Mandle will look asconce at any man using a candle that is not scented with "Man Scents" such as Swarfega, guitars, gunpowder or the sweat of Chuck Norris. In fact if they see a bloke use a plain or girly scented candle they will be very put out, nae quite de-lighted.

Mandle's divine consort is the deity Jillette, who is the best Mandle can get. (Jillette known for being both a little unstable and a little unstubble. She will reveal the goddess in you, but she is also likely to cut you.) ✂

KU KLUX NAN

Goddess of Racist Biddies

Ku-Klux-Nan is a truly ancient goddess. She's 5987 you know, and she can remember a time before we had any of this nonsense. Much of what we know of the origin of this goddess has come down to us through the surviving writings of the 4th BCE writer Xenophobe. In the days when there was but one pantheon known in the world, Ku-Klux-Nan was the Goddess of Quiet Lives. The first time she encountered a deity from another land, she was overcome by fear and jealousy. "How dare they come over here stealing our worshippers!" This vitriol was so powerful that it warped her very form into that of a wizened hag with a mouth like a cat's arse. It is said by some that she was rendered so hideous that she henceforth covered her fearsome visage with a white hood. Others say that she is wearing it because she just had a wash and set done and it's drizzling. Ku-Klux-Nan has numerous children and grandchildren. They are all hideously embarrassed by her when she goes on about politics.

The religion of Ku-Klux-Nan, presided over by High Priestess Hatie Cockpins, is an isolationist one. They associate very rarely with those outside the faith, and then only for the purposes of WTO free trade. A highly judgemental sect, their disapproval is usually expressed through glares, snide comments, boycotting, marching and funding right wing politics. Occasionally they are driven to smite people with a flaming, rolled up copy of the Daily Fail. The clergy live on a strict diet of gammon and each other's opinions. Followers of Ku-Klux-Nan believe that when the righteous die, they will go to a Utopian afterlife, which is just like what England wasn't really like in the 1950s (See: Isle of White).

Surprisingly, amongst Ku-Klux-Nan's followers you will sometimes find elderly members of the long-standing immigrant community. They are there to complain about the latest lot to arrive and how they are ruining everything. They may even win the grudging acceptance of the other church members, provided they can whip up a satisfactory Victoria Sponge for the Garden Fete and don't have too strong an accent. Having them around proves that the other members of the faith are not racist but...

The Temple of Ku-Klux-Nan is essentially a massive echo chamber. Amongst other things it houses a protest placard production workshop, but not a single dictionary. It can be found nestled in England's green and pleasant land for 8 months of the year. Every November the Temple fully relocates to Benidorm for 4 months.

They go well prepared with proper British provisions so that no foreign muck has to be consumed, and a proper cup of tea is assured. To them "foreign muck" is the number one cause of food poisoning and the only way they are going to crush garlic is beneath the heels of their fleece lined jackboots. Whilst there, they will entertain themselves by continually complaining about the locals.

Every March they migrate back to the UK in a ritual pilgrimage known as "Taking Our Country Back". (Outside observers often comment that it was a bit daft for them to leave it lying around unattended in the first place.) ✄

GARDENIA

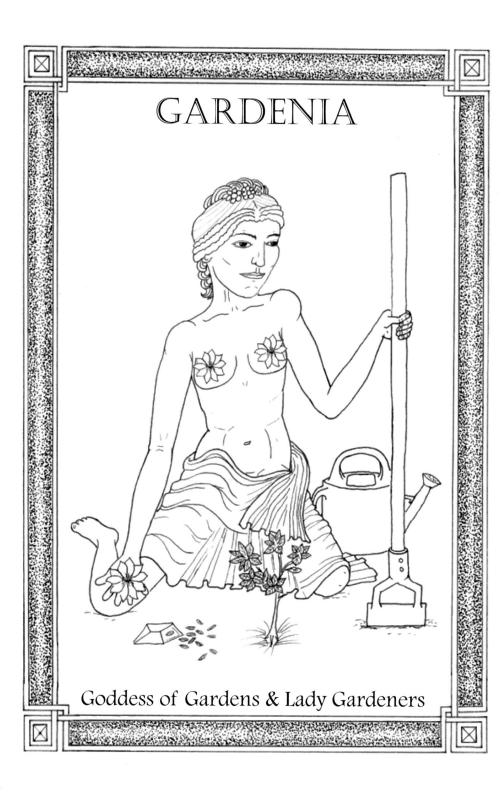

Goddess of Gardens & Lady Gardeners

G ardenia is a Goddess for the dawning of the age of Asparagus. She's a deity you can really dig. Her shapely avatar disguises a Titanium alloy spine with a hinge in it. Her a-maize-ing beauty is renowned. It is said that she walks naked through gardens in the quiet beauty of the night. In the morning you will know you have been blessed with a visitation as your apples will have blushed red and your courgettes will have transformed into marrows. She flies through the skies on her steed "The Snap Dragon".

Gardenia's enemies are the Gnome of Loam (who went insane in the Plantain) who rides the Dandy Lion (who's roots run deep into prehistory). They are said to be trying to bring the winds and frosts that burn the blossoms, and flowers that never bloom are believed to be a very bud omen.

The Temple of Gardenia is home to many wonders. The temple itself is an 8×12 summer-house and is surrounded by a picturesque and well tended lady-garden with an immaculately topiaried bush. The garden is always lush, well watered by the perspiration of the acolytes. If you visit, be sure to marvel at the lawn which yields exactly one grass box of cuttings at each mowing and the shed which always has the tool you need right at the front. The visit is traditionally concluded by visiting their "Museum of Hoes" and casting ones seed upon the ground in offering. If you are tempted to steal from or desecrate the temple, be warned! All the flowers have pistols.

The Temple is populated and run by the Sisters of Gardenia. They are distinguishable by their wearing of the traditional green tights or "Garden Hose". There is a scholarly element to membership of the Sisters of Gardenia. The priestesses will typically study STEM subjects.

In one corner of the temple grounds, a plot is reserved where they are intending to inter the remains of Donald Trump when the time comes. The more free spirited members of the Sisterhood are hoping that if they plant him they can grow their own dope. The Sisters often invite visitors to assist in the care of the gardens. So don't be surprised if you get invited to do a little forking.

The Sisters work to try and ensure every visitor to the temple finds a little inner peas. If you are pensive, one of the Sisters of Gardenia will offer you a peony for your thoughts. They believe gardening to be a panacea for all kinds of mental distress. For example, an often recommended remedy for self-pity is to grow a pear. Many a lost soul has blossomed in their care. The Sisters, who employ music in their healing rituals, are often known to turnip the beet. The most popular hymn is "Don't Stop Be-Leafing". A small libation of wine is offered to the Goddess at each healing ritual, this is always a fine rosé.

The High Priestess of Gardenia takes a managerial role. This, essentially, means the kind of gardening that involves sitting in a deckchair, wearing a big straw hat, drinking Pimms and telling someone else where to dig. The current incumbent is a lady from the West Midlands called "Orchid". The correct way to formally address her is "Yo Orchid!". She is known for being a reckless driver and has often been known to put the petal to the metal on her way to the garden centre and floret home again. ✄

PHARAROAH

God of Petit Fours

Phararoah is the god of tiny confectioneries served after classy dinners. He was one of the rulers of the Rocher Dynasty. His tomb, a pyramid of golden balls, is an architectural marvel of the ancient world. After his death and apotheosis he became the ambassador of the gods.

He is attended by a harem of affluent, elegant and accomplished goddesses to ensure he always comes in a posh box.

The Temple of Phararoah is located beyond the dessert. The temple itself is made of clear Perspex so that the sacred golden balls within can be seen from outside. Their "Hall of Petit Fours" is a place of wondermint. As you enter the temple, a sentient confectionery by the door will greet you and say something flattering.

This surprising entity is known as the "Complimentary Chocolate". Whilst usually benevolent, if incited he has been known to scream "Do you want a piece of me!" at the luckless fool who has upset him. Services, rites and rituals in the temple of Phararoah are always held in the evening and begin after eight. At twilight.

Surprisingly, a small shrine to Phararoah can be found in almost every petrol station and convenience store around the country. These are provided for your convenience so that you can pray frantically for help in over 32,000 easily accessible locations when you realise you've forgotten Grandma's birthday.

The priesthood of Phararoah dress in instantly recognisable, crinkly, golden, metallic robes. They wear brown pleated cup shaped shoes on their feet, and a small oval sticker on their heads. They are often comely, and are considered eye candy by some. The priests run a dating service for their followers. They are reputed to be excellent matchmakers. (Their most recent success being the marriage between the Honourable Miss Elizabeth Shaw and Mr Bendick of Mayfair.)

The prospective groom will give the object of his affection a wafer thin chocolate mint in a tiny black paper envelope. If his suit is successful, she will return this envelope containing a secret note of her affection. The most renowned member of Phararoah's priesthood from history was Mahatma Candhi, who was known for campaigning against oppression and violence powerfully and with confection.

Followers of Phararoah have their own lexicon. They will usually favourably describe things as "Mint" and one of their favourite sayings is "A waist is a terrible thing to mind". If you have been a superlative host to your Phararoahian friend they will say "You are really spoiling us!".

CHOLESTEROLIA

Goddess of Fry-Ups

The saviour of the manual worker, the long distance HGV driver and the hung-over. Cholestrolia is usually considered to be a Goddess of the morning, but is actually welcome at any time of day. Cholesterolia is particularly popular in Scotland, Ireland and Benidorm.

Way back in the mists of antiquity, the goddess was enraged by a mortal swineherd who spied upon her popping to the corner shop in her pyjamas early one morning. In vengeance she caused jets of fire to sprout from the earth and gently incinerate his whole herd of pigs (and some unfortunate mushrooms that just happened to be growing nearby). Drawn by the delicious smell, the other deities gathered round to share the very first fry up in history.

Cholestrolia's divine consort is the God Lard. Worshippers of Cholestrolia sometimes pray to him too in desperate times. Usually with the words, "Lard have mercy!" You will often see the couple rendered together in Cholestrolian sacred artworks.

In the early days of her church, two distinct orders emerged. The "Red Saucers" and the "Brown Saucers". The "Brown Saucers" then schismed further into the "HPs" and the "Daddies". In South Yorkshire there is a heretical break away sect called the "Hendos".

Her temples are known as "Dicula Pinguia". Inside worshippers can partake of the service and shared meal sat on plastic chairs at Formica tables. The Priests and Priestesses are typically surly and robed in symbolically stained vestments. Religious literature is freely available, in tabloid format. On her altar stands a display of condiments, crisps, chocolate and cans. Adjacent to this is the offertory jar hopefully labelled "Tips". The walls are adorned with scriptures listing the permitted foods, with no regard to the correct usage of any known human language. If you pass the door you might hear the sound of a meditation chant drifting out on the breeze "Oooooooooommmmmlette". Every ritual ends by offering a toast to the goddess. With marmalade.

In recent years the faith of Cholestrolia seems to have become slightly less fashionable, perhaps due to pressure from continental religions. However, somehow, those who stray end up wandering back into one of her temples sooner or later. Drawn by the irresistible aroma of frying bacon.

There are certain sins which are considered deadly to followers of Cholesterolia. Chief amongst these are; letting smashed avocado anywhere near your fry up, garnishing with anything green, asking for hippy teas, and serving said fry up on anything other than a proper plate. Muesli is an anathema. Transgressors will be beaten until they are scrambled. (White pudding, Lorne sausage, lava bread, potato cakes, oat cakes and soda bread are all accepted regional variations.)

Her holy day is Fry-day. ✳

MASCARA

The Gothic Deity

Mascara is an anthropomorphic personification of darkness and degradation with flawless eyeliner. Mascara is more Goth than thou will ever be. They are said to have originated in the mysterious forests and mountains of north eastern Europe, the offspring of Captain Sensible (God of The Damned) and Siouxsie (Goddess of Backcombing and Singing on The Roof).

Mascara's temple is a macabre confection of pointed arches and carved skulls in a secret location near Whitby. It is a Temple of Love. It shines like thunder and cries like rain. Dribbly candles flutter in sconces on the walls casting deep, mysterious shadows. The only well illuminated part of the temple is the sacred mirror. All the furniture is designed by the Bauhaus school. In the heart of the Temple is a large console with hundreds of push switches. They don't do anything. The Emos just like to sit at it and depress the buttons. The structure of the temple is supported by a frame of steel girders. Recently, the temple required major restoration. When they consulted an expert structural steel engineer from Sheffield, he looked at the girders and said "Hey now! Hey now now! Look at this corrosion sithee!"

The priesthood wear black at all times, (well, until they find a darker colour). Subtle differences in dress denote membership of different orders such as; The Perkies, The Cybers, The Romantics, The Phetishists and The Steamers. Many wear the "corset of penance". They haven't necessarily done anything particularly bad, they just like it. They each carry a ceremonial "wand" (which is in fact more like a brush on a stick). During rituals of Mascara, the priesthood adopt a strange facial expression, their eyes wide and mouth hanging agape as they gaze into the scared mirror. The sacred mirror is installed in the bathroom, so that the toilet can just be seen in it. Sometimes people gazing into the sacred mirror hallucinate and think they see a monster climbing out of the toilet behind them. (When this happened to me I exclaimed, "Loo Creature!" at my reflection.)

Worshippers of Mascara were hunted and persecuted throughout much of history. In crueller times, heathen mobs (or "Townies") would attempt to trap and castrate the male members of the faith. They would then hang the testes up in their wardrobes as a charm to ward off cloth eating vermin. This is why, in days of yore, Townies tended to smell of Goth Balls.

Before attending worship at Mascara's temple for the first time, it is wise to practice the four key ritual dance moves to avoid scorn from the initiated. They are called; "The Big Fish", "The Little Fish", "The Cardboard Box" and the "Yoyo Trick-Shot".

The first and only commandment of Mascara is, "Don't make me cry!". ✄

GORGONZOLA

Goddess of Cheese Dreams
(one look will drive you crackers)

Gorgonzola is a terrifying ancient deity of the realm of nightmares, worshipped across the five counties and beyond. Her popularity is inter-Comte-nental. One look at Gorgonzola is said to drive you crackers. Completely Emmental. Her snarling visage is webbed with blue veins and she carries a vicious hooked knife and cheese wire. Gorgonzola has spawned numerous lactic phantasm offspring known as "The Little Baby Cheeses". She rides a mythical steed called the "Care-Filly" Her sacred animals are the Welsh Rabbit and the Laughing Cow, and the Primula is her holy flower.

Following Gorgonzola is a whey of life. Every morning her followers must perform a ritual whereby they stand directly in front of a mirror, look into their own eyes, raise their right hand in a gesture of greeting and chant "Hallou me". When on a ship, her followers must partake in a ceremony where they gather on the left side of the boat and raise their hands to their heads in reverence. This is known as the Port Salute. Once a year they hold a competitive cheese eating contest know as "The Cheddar Gorge". It may sound like fun, but even the most voracious competitor usually caves eventually, when they camembert it any more.

Her innermost circle is a shamanistic cult. Her followers will consume large quantities of specially prepared dairy products to induce a transcendental nightmare state. There are special preparation rites for making these "dark cheeses" where Edam is made backwards. I am told that performing these rituals is a bit of a strain.

The senior priest can be recognised by his great height. He is not, in fact, tall. He just always has his sacred stilt on. The priesthood wear muslin robes and necklaces strung with tiny bells. They did experiment with making vestments from cheese slices, but it didn't work. They discovered that, when you try to wear it, fromage frays. One of the daily duties of the clergy is to call the faithful to prayer by ringing their baby bells.

Her shrine is located near Wensleydale in a complex system of well-guarded natural caves. This means worshippers must pick their way past a rock fort and across a lot of de-brie to get to it. Then they must cross a circular lake of stringy molten cheese which surrounds the shrine, known as the "Moatzarella". Deep within the shrine is a statue of Gorgonzola. In order to make the statue survive the damp cave conditions the priests painted it. (In fact they double glossed her.)

The motto of Gorgonzola's followers is, "A Dolcelatte is for life, not just for Christmas."

Gorgonzola was Christianised in the 5th Century CE as St. Agur. ✗

(Sorry if all these cheese jokes are nacho cup of tea. I'm only Paulin your leg.)

SHIVA ME TIMBERS

God of Nautical Clichés

The philosophy of the faith of Shiva Me Timbers is to fill the void of taste, interests or design skill in one's life with generic sea themed crap. The theory is that this will imply to others that you are an adventurous, salty sea dog with the wealth and time to explore the world (between your shifts at the call centre). Parrots, West Country accents and casual sexual morals are all encouraged. For worshippers of Shiva Me Timbers, every day is "Talk Like a Pirate Day". Acolytes with at least one prosthetic limb are considered blessed, as they will always have a gruesome, ripping yarn to tell.

If you commit a serious transgression of the faith of Shiva-Me-Timbers, you may be sentenced to "roll the plank". Shiva-Me-Timbers is an equal opportunities faith, and all their planks are wheelchair accessible.

There are many majestic temples to Shiva Me Timbers. They sail the seven seas to spread the word of the god. If you visit any port town, you will see one schooner or later. The temples are always immaculately maintained, as they like to keep things ship shape. Each one has a Shivan Temple Cat for vermin control. Shivan Temple Cats are a rare breed with 9 tails. Inside they are decorated with canvas upholstery, rope-work storage baskets, driftwood, lifebelts and badly taxidermied seagulls. You can create the nautical temple look in your own home. Everything you need is available from "AYE IKEA".

The clergy of Shiva Me Timbers can be recognised by their tattoos, blue trousers and stripy shirts (known as "Bristol Fashion"). Membership of the priesthood is open to both buoys and girls equally. There are often heated theological arguments amongst them about the merits of steam ships versus sail. This schism is known as the Great Mast Debate. The current High Priest is a permanently jovial man called Roger. He has lived his whole life in religious service. He started out as the cabin boy. As a money maker, the church of Shiva Me Timbers run a sperm bank. They are renowned for their able semen.

The rituals of Shiva Me Timbers always begin with the weighing of the anchor on the ceremonial scales. Sadly, due to the traditional consumption of rum, they usually end with everyone keeling over, utterly wrecked with all souls lost.

VERRUCA

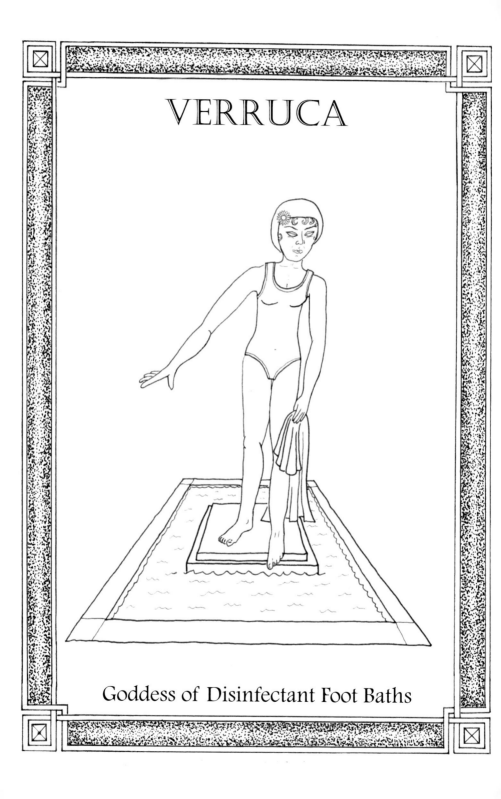

Goddess of Disinfectant Foot Baths

Verruca is a deity from ancient history. She popped up shortly after the invention of the Roman Bath and has hung around for 3000 years. Once the sacred pools of Verruca were a common sight in public baths across the world. Nowadays her popularity is diminished and they are a rarer sight. Modern practices have frozen Verruca out. Worship of Verruca is now considered to be somewhat old fashioned and corny, but she still has the ability to make a splash.

Verruca has three avatars. First is the stunningly beautiful Mermaid (she just washed up like this), the bountiful Mermother and the wise and ancient Mercrone. Her consort is Speedo - God of Illegal Budgie Trafficking. Her arch enemy is the demon "Mankini".

The Priests and Priestesses of Verruca also known as "The Life Guards" can be recognised by their skin tight Lycra vestments, the neat rubber caps that completely conceal their hair, the whistles hung around their necks and their pink eyes. All devotees, not just the priesthood, wear the sacred rubber sock of protection. The daily routine of a devout Verruca worshipper begins with a race at dawn to place their towel on the best sun lounger.

Verruca has a dark and strange mythology. Ancient historians recorded grizzly rites where human body parts were sacrificed to her. She was said to particularly favour offerings of athlete's feet. Verrucan parents used to frighten their children into obedience with tales of a tribe of uncivilised and unhygienic barbarians known as "The Wild Swimmers", who eschewed Verruca's sacred pools and leaped fearlessly into any stretch of open water.

Modern worship is much less macabre and more enjoyable. One can float in her sacred waters and use your noodle to meditate on spiritual matters. In the back ground, the temple musicians (known as "The Arm Band") will serenade you. It is customary to take a pound coin to Verruca's temple as an offering when you visit. Please place your contribution in the slot on your locker.

Following the way of Verruca is said to be good for the sole. It is also said to be good for the body as her temple is a place of heeling. The 9 commandments that acolytes strive to adhere to are;

1. *Thou shalt not run.*
2. *Thou shalt not push.*
3. *Thou shalt not perform gymnastics or acrobatics.*
4. *Thou shalt not shout.*
5. *Thou shalt not duck.*
6. *Thou shalt not engage in heavy petting.*
7. *Thou shalt not bomb.*
8. *Thou shalt not swim in the diving area.*
9. *Thou shalt not smoke.*

Now her popularity has waned, her priesthood run a breakdown service on the side called "Toe Trucks" to raise money to repair the temple's fallen arches. ✂

WING & DING

Gods of Fonts

These ancient deities originate in the Far East, as did the art of woodblock printing. They are found in variations in other pantheons, sometimes as a single being. For example, they were known in Ancient Greece as ΣΨΜΒΟΛ. A version of them did eventually make it into the Roman Pantheon, but it was not until just before Christianisation, in times new. All in all they are said to be pretty cool deities, and they are known to rock well. However, they can become vengeful if angered and have been known to make terror strike through hearts. Wing & Ding are said to have each been reincarnated three times before their apotheosis. These subtly different avatars are known as Wing & Ding One, Two and Three. Wing's sacred animal is the Dingbat. Ding's sacred animal is Webding the Spider.

The Temples of Wing & Ding are decorated with the mysterious holy symbols painted on every surface. Newer modern temples will usually be constructed with a slight slant to the architecture, known as the Italic style. Older temples will usually be built in a more traditional Gothic style. Within each temple is a giant stone bowl which houses the temple's copies of the sacred texts. This is known as the "Font of All Knowledge". The sacred texts, known collectively as "The Superscript" are written in a code comprised of 94 hieroglyphic symbols. They are only decipherable by the priesthood and theological scholars following many years of study. These divine words of Wing and Ding were said to have originally been delivered to mankind by courier. The texts are never completely translated into the western alphabet. However, small excerpts are printed in Trebuchet font on launch materials for new church projects.

The heavenly consorts of Wing and Ding are the Eight Sisters of Lucida. As a result polygamy is permitted within this faith, and some followers prefer to practice this open type of relationship. Sadly, the faith is not always understood by outsiders, and followers of Wing & Ding sometimes experience discrimination. They go into business establishments only to be told "We don't serve your type here". The priests of Wing & Ding are dedicated typophiles known as "Serifs". The priestesses are in charge of the punctuation (as only they have periods). In recent years the whole faith has been administered from near Mansfield in the UK. Therefore the highest ranking priest holds the title of "Serif of Nottingham". The current incumbent is Sir Harrington Copperplate -Gothic-Bold (who I am told is Cambria educated). Tragically his predecessor, the Liverpudlian Ar Julian, was assassinated. To this day the crime was never solved and no one knows who shot the Serif. In return for a donation to the temple, the Serifs will supply you with a prophetic scroll, printed in Futura. If appealed to, the Serifs may also hold a court and dispense with legal matters. However, they only mete out punishment when it is fully justified. One traditional penance given is to live solely on Kern Flakes for a set period.

The nemesis of Wing and Ding is the trickster demon "Comic Sans". Falling into the trap of Comic Sans is said to be the fate of the immoral and unimaginative. Followers of Wing & Ding believe that those who live an unimaginative life will go to a dark underworld called "Helvetica" when they die. Some mystics of the faith believe they know the secret to everlasting life and youth. They believe that the secret to eternal life is ✂︎♎︎□︎■︎♓︎♦︎ ♎︎⑂︎♏︎✂︎🖉︎   ✖︎

RARARA

God of Cheerleaders

Need a little motivation to get you through Hump Day? Then RaRaRa could be the deity for you. He's the God that's always cheering you on to be your best.

The Temple of RaRaRa is built around the sacred waters of the Hand Spring (which is about half a mile from the Summer Salt Mines). The compound is planted with an impressive orchard of a unique variety of apple tree. These grow an unusual "double apple" fruit and are known as Pomme-Pommes. The temple building has four wings with a rectangular central courtyard. This inner courtyard is known as the Squadwrangle, and it is where training and larger scale worship takes place. The roof of the temple is adorned with many decorative aerials.

His temples have (possibly) the most entertaining rituals of any faith. The rites always follow a strict routine. The priesthood will guide you in waving your sacred pompoms and lead you in a rousing chorus of "Give him an R! Give him an A!"

Conducting the worship is arduous for the clergy. So, before worship commences they will traditionally drink some root beer. At the most hallowed part of the ritual, worshippers will share the Holy Hot Dog and all partake of a sip of soda from the JumboMegaCup. During a short break, a guest minister will usually perform a hymn as a kind of half time show. Afterwards, as you leave, be sure to pick up a souvenir from the "Tuck Shop".

There is a large seminary college where postulates are trained for religious service. The first thing they learn is that cheering is a serious athletic endeavour. They must be prepared to exceed those they support in gymnastic prowess. They are also taught to expect and forbear low wages and a general lack of respect. Students are kept company by a friendly ghost who inhabits the building, known affectionately as "The School Spirit". The college uniform colour is yeller.

There is a dark chapter in the history of the faith of RaRaRa. Originally the holy pompoms used in worship were made from the pelt of the Wild PomPom (Latin name *Lanae globus*) a long coated, woolly beast. Sadly, these have now been hunted to extinction, and today the pompoms used in worship are made from imitation synthetic fibres.

The church of RaRaRa rarely involves itself in politics. When they have ventured into the hustings, their candidates have been known to flip flop.

Members of this faith will often save all their lives to be interred in the largest human pyramid possible after death. Followers will often involve themselves in the study of astronomy throughout life as they believe that after death, the journey to the afterlife takes us to become one with the heavens. They believe that potentially we are All-Stars. ✳

MADHUR

Goddess of the Great British Curry

Gentle Goddess of British Curries, Writers, Travellers and Actresses, Madhur is a Jack of all trades and a Master of Naan. She originated when the people of late 20th century Britain realised that their food was monotonous bland crap and they desperately needed, "Some of that foreign muck," to stave off the culinary ennui.

Madhur was their saviour from the east, from the silver screen to the soup tureen. Now she is truly taken into their hearts.

You will almost certainly be first drawn to Madhur's temple (or Dawat) by the delicious cooking aromas. Don't be too shy to tikka look inside. Any visitor knocking at her temple door is warmly invited to cumin. You may want to wear an extra layer of clove-ing, it can be a little chilli inside. It is traditional for visitors to her temple to leave an offering of Biryani, known as the "Sacrifrice".

Madhur is served by both priests and priestesses, known as "Madhur's Dhalings". The priesthood usually live in the temple where they each have a madras to sleep on with a pilau to rest their head. Priests traditionally wear tiny tight swimming trunks beneath their vestments, known as "Bhaji Smugglers". This is why they always sit down gingerly. When the High Priestess is feeling a little down, the other priestesses will play some of the music of Karnataka to pep her up. The priesthood have recently developed an new kind of otter curry, known as a Tarka Massalla. It is not for neophytes. It you eat this dish without first acclimatising your digestive system, you'll end up with a medical condition known as the "Ring of Shite Water".

This is a religion characterised by a positive attitude to life amongst its devotees. In fact, they see positivity as the ghee to success. They also believe in the balance of energy in the universe, or "Korma". Followers of Madhur will cheerfully greet each other with a warm "Aloo!". When something needs doing, they do it raita way, it is frowned upon to just sit around on your anise. When under stress they do their best to keep calm and karahi on. ✄

(All jokes above are a warm homage and intended Indiabsolute nicest possible way. No otters were curried or otherwise harmed in the making of this cartoon.)

ELVISH

God of Tribute Acts

W henever a legend dies and leaves a musical legacy, Elvish will send one of his followers to keep their memory alive. His followers believe that, if they devote their lives to honouring their chosen bard, after their own death they will go to heaven, known to them as Graceland. They try to pursue their spiritual journey whilst defending their faith against suspicious minds. Neophytes begin their journey as members of the "Tribute Audience" for the higher ranking acolytes.

Followers are welcomed from all walks of life. Perhaps remembering that Elvish himself had unusually humble beginnings. His parents were lowly hearth gods of baking, and he was born in the gateaux.

The Temples of Elvish have brightly lit, attention grabbing, frontages with neon signboards. His largest and chief Temple is located in Las Vegas. This temple houses many sacred relics such as the original "Jailhouse Rock", the holy Teddy Bear and a huge collection of Good Luck Charms. The Temple is actually built around an ancient tree which forms the wooden heart of the structure.

If you visit his Temple you may get to hear a rendition of one of Elvish's most well known hymns, it goes "Sing Hosanna to the King, Baby." On your visit you may also get the honour of meeting current High Priest of Elvish, Mr Amaal Shoukup. If you need guidance you can consult the Pelvic Oracle who also resides in the temple. You won't find Elvish himself there though. Elvish has left the building.

The Priesthood can be recognised by their distinctive white vestments adorned with precious gems of Rhine Zirconia. They move softly around the compound in their blue suede shoes. Every day they devote many hours to vocal training, dressmaking and floor exercises which focus on the pelvic area.

The priesthood run a wide range of eateries to raise funds for their church and costumes. These range from the humble "Ain't Nothin' but a Hotdog"* and "The Wonder of Stew" to the Michelin starred "Art Steak Hotel**". All provide excellent quality fare, and are recommended to those who love meat tender. All these eateries celebrate an annual festival of Elvish where they give away free fruit. So be sure to visit one on "Unchained Melon Day". Not all catering ventures are run by the priesthood though, some chefs fraudulently claim membership. There's a guy works down our chip shop who swears he's Elvish, but he's a liar.

Be sure to welcome Elvish into your life. Thanks to his followers he is available for Birthdays, Weddings and Bar Mitzvahs. Oh yeah. Uh huh huh. Thankyouverymuch. ✄

*If you want to be cryin' all the time, onions are extra.
** Why yes! It IS down at the end of a lonely street.

SEMOLINA

Goddess of School Dinners

Semolina watches over all forms of institutional food whether in schools, workplaces, hospitals or prisons. Basically, anywhere that barely non-toxic dull grey slop is doled out onto plastic trays. Semolina ensures a place in paradise for those who clear their own tray. Fryday is her holy day, when chips are served.

Her temple is furnished with long tables, metal water jugs and stackable plastic chairs. The high altar resembles a long counter. It may well be the only altar to feature a sneeze guard. Her priestesses stand behind the altar to deliver the service. Above the altar the acronym S.U.A.E.I.* is inscribed in chalk on a blackboard, along with the two choices for that day's fare; take it or leave it. A typical rite lasts around half an hour and involves 25 minutes of queuing and 5 minutes to scoff down a sacrament.

Behind the scenes the signature "barely non-toxic dull grey slop" is created by processing vast quantities of fungus. This takes place in the mush room. Salads are also served (the other vegetable choice on offer is ketchup). It is considered very auspicious to find a caterpillar in your salad (as it shows that it's real). It is considered a very bad omen to find half a caterpillar in your salad.

Priestesses of Semolina can be recognised by the wearing of the Holy Hair-net of Cantina. They undergo rigorous training every day of the week, including learning to make ice cream in little plastic pots at sundae school. One should always treat the priests and priestesses of Semolina with great deference and respect as they will be touching your food and deciding your portion. People who transgress from correct behaviour within the temple will be sent to the back of the line.

The Priestesses are also the keepers of the sacred texts. These hold the secrets of the faith, such as the recipes for pink custard and chocolate concrete. It is not known why, when the entrees are so inedible, the desserts should be so delicious. It may just be that after their corned beef hash, even a nine volt battery would taste like ambrosia.

This is not entirely the clergy's fault. There is said to be a pernicious secret governing circle of Semolina's cult. They meet in a plush dining room by the side of the Thames in London and brutally cut the budgets of Semolina's temples whilst enjoying a free five course banquet with Port and exotic cheeses. Recently, they have cut the wages and benefits of the priestesses who ladle up the gravy and custard by a capitalist practice known as out-saucing.

The ethos of the faith of Semolina is that all within an institution will be united in solidarity by the hatred of the food. From the pupils, through the IT department who drop in for a quick byte, to the Maths teachers who come for a meal[2]. They are all bonded in a universal loathing and so community spirit is fostered. Some say that following the way of Semolina is a piece of cake…

…but only if you've finished your vegetables. ✄

* Shut up and eat it.

THESAURUS

God of Saying Things a Different way

A voluble, loquacious, articulate, effusive, garrulous, chatty, eloquent, gabby, verbose, vocal and multiloquent deity. Devotees of Thesaurus are never lost for words. Thesaurus used to be the lover of Apostrophe, the Goddess of Punctuation. However, this relationship ended when she became too possessive. In his mythos Thesaurus lives high above the clouds on Mount Weasel.

The cult of Thesaurus is very secretive. The first rule of the Order of Thesaurus is that you do not talk about, speak, mention, chat, discuss, shoot the breeze or chin-wag about the Order of Thesaurus. Therefore it is not known for sure who the current high priest of Thesaurus is, but there are speculations that it may be Susie Dent. Historians hotly disputed whether their first High Priest was Peter Roget or Dr Samuel Johnson.

In the heart of the temple of Thesaurus sits their holy book, placed upon a velvet cushion on a marble pedestal. Just over a hundred years ago a terrible sacrilegious crime was committed when someone stole the holy book, but there was no public outcry. People were left with no words to describe how angry they were.

The priesthood break their fast at dawn every day with a Synonym Roll. They are delicious, just like grammar used to make. They then spend the day in the sombre study of lexicography. They have made many great advances in this field, including inventing the word "Plagiarism". They also discovered that the ancient version of our alphabet originally only had 25 letters, but no one knew why.

Over time the priesthood have given in to the fact that their works are mainly used for looking up profanities. Recently they have published several specialised reference volumes to meet this demand. These include the “Dicktionary”, the “Sexicon”, and the “Fuckabulary”. These tomes are notable for being the only reference works teenagers will use voluntarily.

If you see a priest of Thesaurus, dancing and flailing wildly, go to his aid and help him shake out his robes. He probably has an antonym. (They really go for the synonym roll crumbs).

Thesaurus was later Christianised as St Poecilonym.

CANCELLE

Goddess of Public Transport

Cancelle watches over all those who chose to take their spiritual journey in close communion with others from all walks of life. She is appealed to by those who wait in the rain or stand in the aisles. Some say that worship of Cancelle is the preserve of the less financially fortunate. However, she also has affluent devotees who believe following her way has benefits for the whole planet. The way of Cancelle is considered by many to be the most environmentally friendly method of getting to the afterlife. Devotees of Cancelle believe that, when they die, they will travel to the next world on a brand new, clean Omnichariot. (The Omnichariot is a high occupancy vehicle which will always move twice as fast when you are trying to catch it as when you are in it). The scriptures say that (for the righteous) it will arrive on time and will be of the correct operating company to accept the Day-Mega-Soul-Saver ticket you purchased earlier. If one has lived an especially devout life, one will travel to the afterlife without having to share a seat or hold a conversation with a fruitcake.

In antiquity her temples used to be known as "Stations". However, in the 21st Century they have been trendily rebranded as "Interchanges". They are cavernous halls filled with the aromas of the traditional diesel fume and urine incense. The readings and sermon are delivered in an ethereal echoic voice through a crackly P.A. system. Although delivered at great volume and in received pronunciation, it is impossible to decipher any useful information. The service will begin with a cry of "Hold tight please" and will end with the ringing of a small bell. There is almost always inadequate seating in the temples, to ease this issue one should move down to the back of the temple on entering. In getting to the back of the temple one can fall over 50 feet with only minor injuries. You should not attempt to sit in one of the "priority seats" at the front unless you have genuine need of them. Transgressors of this rule will be condemned to die the "Death of a Thousand Walking Sticks".

There are some strict rules you must abide by if you wish to visit one of Cancelle's houses of worship. Consumption of alcohol is forbidden within the temple, also loud music, skateboarding and putting your feet on the seats. Worshippers are constantly reminded not to leave baggage unattended and to report suspicious packages (so you are advised not to wear Speedos when visiting). If you are in need of refreshment during your visit, most of her temples feature a café serving tea and the customary holy trinity of foods; the Pious Pasty, the Sacred Sausage Roll and the Transcendental Teacake. Smaller shrines and chapels are known as "Stops" or "Halts" and may consist of little more than a holy sign on a chewing gum encrusted pole. These are often situated in bleak and isolated places, serving the homesteads of a few remote faithful. If a statue of Cancelle in the temple gets broken, they have a replacement bust service.

The High Priest of each temple is known as the "Driver", and they are assisted by their deputy, known as the "Conductor". (In the higher Maglev Temples, this post is called the "Superconductor".) As one leaves the temple, one must express one's thanks or be considered an ill-mannered oaf by all aboard.

The scriptures of Cancelle are revised at least once annually in order to maintain some mystery in the faith. However, the tradition of having a long period of inactivity at some point in the day followed by three services back to back, is always preserved. The days on which the new scriptures are adopted are invariably days of chaos. Cancelle appears in numerous pantheons around the world and is also sometimes known as Tramantha and in Wales as Bend-Y-Bus. She is also the Goddess of Monorails, but I couldn't think of any one-liners about that. ✄

BRABANTIA

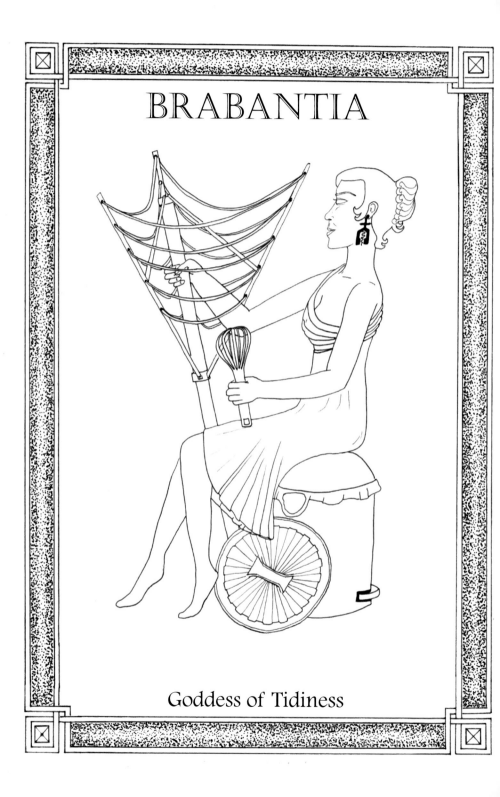

Goddess of Tidiness

Brabantia is the goddess of tidiness. She is the reason all the other deities are able to sport immaculate and crisp white robes every day and sip their nectar from sparkling clean chalices.

She has the most immaculate temples with a place for everything and everything in its place. The walls are lined floor to ceiling with shelves of storage caddies full of utensils. The grounds are gaily adorned with rotary prayer airers, which spin gently in the wind. Perhaps the most striking feature of the temple is the collection of 288 waste bins of every size and hue.

Followers of Brabantia believe that carrying out mundane household chores induces a transcendental meditative state through which wisdom and insight may be gained. Sacred music is used to accompany these tasks, and help achieve the desired state of mind. Her most famous hymn is “Another One Fights the Dust”.

Worshippers of Brabantia have important traditions for life’s rites of passage. A new-born Brabantian will be initiated into the faith by a priest who will don the “Gloves of Marigold” and then briefly dip the child in a font of foamy dishwater. When Brabantians marry, for the first year the husband will do all the cleaning, because a new groom sweeps cleanest. Upon death followers of Brabantia have their remains neatly stored within the temple. Families can choose between a Roll Top or Fall Front "Dead Bin" in Metallic Mint, Passion Red, Clay Pink or Daisy Yellow.

The vestments of the clergy are always immaculately laundered and pressed. Their cleanliness is inspected before each ritual by a group of 3 senior priests known as "The Ironing Board". They'd better wear them right, a priest who fails to meet the standards will do penance on the "Dish Rack". Despite the threat of this, many youngsters aspire to be priests of Brabantia. One key duty of a priest is to clean the temple mirrors, and this is something a lot of young people can see themselves doing.

There are various sub-sects of Brabantia. One notable order is a desert dwelling group who practice abstinence from alcohol. They are known as “The Dry Cleaners”. All the various groups are overseen by the current High Priest, the Most Hygienic Bruce Springclean. He has absolute authority amongst his flock, everyone knows he’s the boss.

The motto of Brabantia is “Don’t put it down, put it away.”

ANAGLYPTA & ARTEX

God & Goddess of Failed DIY Projects

T he patron deities of "structural decor". These gods have been around a long time, and it is likely to be many more centuries until the last traces of them are removed. Their temple could be a potential death trap. Above it's entrance are carved the words "Texit Hiatum".

In mythology Artex and Anaglypta are husband and wife. Theirs is a passionate and stormy relationship, often fought in the aisles of B&Q. In the end Artex won dominion over the ceilings and Anaglypta won control of the walls below the picture rail. Now, in unison, they cover their realms to hide the cracks in the universe and hold up the lath of the heavens. Before marrying Anaglypta, Artex was romantically linked with the demon Asbestos. Until Asbestos was banished from the realm by the legendary hero Coshh.

As Anaglypta and Artex are a married couple deity, this is reflected in the practices of their sect. You must go through the initiation rite as a couple. There are no requirements regarding gender or marital status, you just have to have a significant other to go through "The Initiation Trial" with. Initiation is not open to anyone with prior practical skills or knowledge. You must be as a blank slate. The initiation begins with both initiates being forced to strip…

…lead based paint and suspicious green Victorian wall paper from a "period property" which they have just impoverished themselves to buy. This is usually a two up two down nineteenth century terraced "villa" that was advertised as "perfect for a first time buyer". As the hapless initiates peel away the paper, the plaster beneath is rigged to fall away from the wall in great chunks. Added to this is the spicy danger that not all the floor joists are load-bearing and some of the curtain rails are. A couple are considered as accepted into the faith once they have returned the property to the appearance of a liveable condition whilst not exceeding their budget by more than 100%. If you are friends with a follower of Anaglypa and Artex, we advise caution when visiting their home. It's probably best not to lean on anything.

In order to advance to the priesthood a couple must undergo an advanced rite where they must furnish their domicile. This involves negotiating a bewildering maze-like show room, followed by an equally bewildering warehouse, followed by lunch in a Swedish café, before driving home in a dangerously loaded car and successfully assembling their purchases. All this must be accomplished without a screaming meltdown, periods of icy silence or random murders. Few pass the test.

Once you are in the sect of Anaglypta and Artex, it is very hard to leave. The only way out is to pay a series of skilled tradespeople to renovate your house to remove every last trace of the presence of the gods. Make sure you hire blessed builders, pious plasterers and sanctified sparkies. Only they can restore your home to a point where another person would not have to be completely insane to buy it.

Artex is a spiky, prickly character. A brush with him is likely to leave you raw and bleeding. Anaglypta always looks slightly tired, old and dusty.

At the festival of Artex it is traditional for worshippers to get plastered. Their most memorable hymn is "What Goes Up" by Gordon & Brown. ✤

THAW

God of Broken Freezers

Wherever the constant background hum falls silent, Thaw is there. Thaw's association with broken appliances probably derives from his tendency to try and mend things with his "mighty hammer". In his mythology Scampi (the God of Mild Mischief) grew fed up with Thaw's percussion engineering and not having any ice for his mead. Also, he “Had a whole box of Magnums in there man!” Enraged, Scampi forced a Crown of Prawns onto Thaw’s head and then perforated him with a shower of falling icicles. Thaw did try to defend himself, but unfortunately he’s a bit of a drip.

Thaw’s temples are usually simple white box-like buildings which have a distressing smell and a large puddle of water outside the front door. Many are upright structures with a single, large front door. Some are low, long and squat and accessed via an opening roof. In the USA the temples have a distinct “double front door” style.

His priests are known for being a bit “snowflake”, in that they will frequently break down and lose their cool. Despite this, they usually maintain themselves in good physical condition. The Elder Priest is said to have the body of an 18 year old, or at least he did until his freezer broke and it went funny. Nonetheless, they are a close knit college, and should you join them, you will make lots of cool friends. The only downside to joining is that the temple DVD collection contains only Frozen and Ice Age.

The great annual festival of Thaw is called “Deliquesce” and it takes place on the day after the first eight hour long power cut of the year. Thawians will cook and eat every scrap of food in their stores in a frenzy "before it goes off", (including that tub of mystery brown liquid and chunks that was probably a homemade soup once upon a time) and a great feast is shared. At Deliquesce Thawian parents will traditionally give their children gifts of fridges. Many parents will sentimentally enjoy watching their little ones’ faces light up as they open them.

Many people have found enlightenment through the way of Thaw. The words “I was blind, but now icy.” are often repeated in his sacred texts and anthems. It is forbidden by Thaw to take a slice of lemon in your drink. When offered ice and lemon at a pub, a Thawian will cry for just ice.

When a Thawian passes away they will be given a traditional funeral by their family. For these events, professional mourners are always hired, known as the “Cry O’re Genics”. Then the deceased is frozen and interred in a sub-zero crypt. All Thawian crypts have the words “Icy Dead People” carved above the entrance door.

People also pray to Thaw when the icebox is taking too frigging long to defrost.

GELATINE

Goddess of Wobbly Puddings

A Goddess set in a perfect mould. One is always certain when one has seen a vision of Gelatine - because Jam don't shake like that. In her mythology she seduces allsorts of unsuspecting mortals to bear an army of children, known as the Geli Babies. She raises and trains these demi-god warriors to fight the demons Aspic and Vegan. She is not a goddess to be trifled with.

Her temples are delicate architectural shells and are sometimes made of plastic, ceramic or glass. However, the highest of her churches are always made of brilliant burnished copper. The shapes vary, but interconnected ascending domes and sweeping arches are common themes. The altar is always laden with a display of delectable dessert offerings. The altar constantly gently oscillates by means of a cunning concealed mechanism. During a typical rite at one of Gelatine's temples, one will partake of a communion of bread and wine gums.

Gelatine has a somewhat rubenesque priesthood. They will daily engage in at least an hour of meditative jiggling. This is said to be quite a sight to see. The High Priestess or Priest is known as "The Great Haribo". The high priest has exclusive access to air travel in the church's Jellycopter which can often be seen wobbling through the sky as The Great Haribo goes about the Goddess' work. The current Great Haribo is called Mr Hartley.

Gelatine is the kind of deity one often finds where one least expects her to be. She has a side-line as a guardian of medicines and washing detergents. However, she can most commonly be found at children's birthday parties. She is not an all powerful deity. She is vulnerable to water, high temperatures and pineapples.

In pre-congregation times she was Christianised and later appropriated by the Roman Catholic Church as St. Blancmange. ✄

AFRODITE

Goddess of Fabulous Hair

frodite is a goddess who knows how to work what her mother gave her. Legend has it that she stepped naked from a seashell. (Although when I tried this I was asked not to come back to the Sealife Centre. Double bloody standards if you ask me).

Afrodite has several different sects that worship her. The Pantenes, The Tresemmes, The Wellas, The Herbalessences and the oldest sect, The Vosenes (who consider themselves head and shoulders above the rest). Regardless of their affiliation, the priests and priestesses wear distinctive long black nylon robes, tied at the neck, which completely cover their other garments. This is topped off with a towel draped around the neck and secured with a plastic hair clip.

You may know her most popular hymn:

She is D divine
She is I incredible
She is S straightening
She is C curling
She is O oh, oh, oh

Key to the observances of all the different sects are the hours spent in meticulous ritual grooming. It is believed that a meditative state of a higher altered consciousness is achieved in the hairdresser's chair. At her temples one can purchase meditation CDs of hairstylist conversation. Such as the classic "Have you had your holiday yet this year?" or "What did you think of last week's Strictly?" to help you achieve this state of nirvana.

At the initiation ceremony into the faith Afrodite, the postulate will be anointed with warm sacred oil, and wrapped in a heated towel for fifteen minutes before being leaned backwards and ritually lathered and rinsed in the font (the last two steps to be repeated as needed). Then a priest or priestess will hold a mirror up behind them to scare away any demons they may be facing. At this juncture the neophyte will speak the words, "Great, cheers, thanks. What do I owe you?"

In every temple, sat along one side, there is a row of between three and five elderly Nuns of Afrodite. Their blue rinsed, curlered heads encapsulated by strange pod-like devices from which a gentle drone can be heard. They sit there all day, as other worshippers come and go, maintaining a state of lowered consciousness by reading Heat Magazine.

Followers of Afrodite believe that when they curl up and dye they will climb the hair-way to heaven, provided they have been virtuous. The unkempt and unvirtuous will be condemned to Hairdes where they will be forced to forever style their Barnet with hair styx.

Afrodite's sacred text is called "The Little Book of Clam".

GRINDR

God of Online Dating

L et's get one thing straight. He's not. Grindr was a hugely popular deity amongst the seafaring Vikings during those long voyages. It can be lonely on the fjords in winter, and the nearest booty call might be across 5 miles of sheer icy mountain. Grindr is the deity who brings lovers together to keep out the cold. Followers of Grindr carry his talisman, which will vibrate when another eligible follower comes within navigable distance. The pattern of vibration delivers important information about this potential hook-up by Norse Code.

Grindr is the son of Blue Tooth. His origin story states that his mother, Nokia, gave birth to him in the closet to hide him from the evil Ice Giant Homophobe. Once fully grown he began to search for his sworn enemy, protecting his anonymity by appearing only as a disembodied torso. Once Homophobe was bound and rendered powerless, Grindr proudly left the closet and the rest of the pantheon had to get used to it. Grindrs has a beloved (mostly) straight twin sister called Tinder. Grindr is said to sail the seven seas in his longboat, called the Pride of Asgard. Its figurehead is a Drag-on. A fabulous and fierce mythical beast.

Following the path of Grindr can be arduous. The standards of lifestyle, diet and dress are high. Many devotees pray assiduously and will check in with Grindr every few minutes. Even though there is nothing new. If Grindr blesses you with finding the perfect partner, it is traditional to celebrate that union until you are both Thor. In his temple, his priests or "Nerdics" tirelessly refine his holy algorithms to ensure appropriate matches. Once a year all followers of Grindr meet up and celebrate their Pride in their faith with parties and parades.

The Temple of Grindr are places where one can be one's true self. The interiors are decorated with impeccable style and taste. The sacred music played there is a rustic traditional style, because there's nowt so queer as folk. On the wall of the shady side of the temple worshippers will often post saucy pictures of themselves as offerings to Grindr in hopes he will favour them with a match with Mr Right (or at least Mr Right Now). Parking is to the rear.

Grindr is, perhaps surprisingly, the only vegetarian Norse God. In fact he's Norvegan. He is famous for his impressively large chopper and smooth shiny helmet. His sacred animals are a handsome bear with a powerful right swipe and a white swallow. ⚒

YAHTZEE

God of Rainy Holidays

Yahtzee originated circa 1945 when the family caravan holiday began to grow in popularity. Picture the scene: you have driven 200 miles to spend a week living in a biscuit tin on wheels and weeing in a bucket. All because the surroundings are marginally prettier than the surroundings at home. However, said bucolic idyll is obscured from view by fog and you are made a prisoner by a maelstrom. In the mind-crushing desperation of boredom, you turn to the board games chest under the couch/bed. To your horror, you discover that Scrabble has no S's, Monopoly only has £5 in the bank and Kerplunk has lost its marbles. But lo! Great joy! The divine salvation of Yahtzee came in answer to your prayers. From the depleted detritus of lesser games, five dice are salvaged and pen and paper found.

Following the way of Yahtzee is traditionally a summer vocation. The temples of Yahtzee are tin tabernacles on wheels of varying sizes, scented with the burning of the sacred Calor Gas stove and smouldering toast incense. The faithful tow their own temple for many miles with underpowered cars on unsuitable roads to gather in groups in fields with a few basic facilities. Large gatherings of Yahtzeeites are often a cause of rage amongst locals and motorists, and have been known to be the victims of hate crime.

Worship takes place in small groups of 1-8 players. The rite is comprised of 13 symbolic rounds. Tea is traditionally drunk throughout to sustain the faithful. However, moderation is recommended as it is considered impolite to interrupt the proceedings for a tea pee. The other sovereign rule that must be adhered to during worship is that the dice must remain in the holy chalice. Persons who transgress and drop the sacred dice will be sent on a guilt trip to empty the porta-potty.

Although worship usually takes place in family units, Yahtzeeites will often visit other groups for a session of prayer. This usually occurs when they can no longer bear the company of their own kin without murder occurring. Through this practice the children of the followers of Yahtzee form new lifetime friendships for a fortnight each year. Excursions for the worship of Yahtzee are usually a carefully planned annual event, but may also be a hasty retreat in times of spiritual crisis.

The priesthood of Yahtzee practice astragalomancy, and one can obtain a reading in return for an offering of nibbles and snacks. What they invariably divine is that one will experience approximately an hour of being mildly entertained before one must again contemplate the bleakness of existence. Physical perfection and health is not required of the clergy. In fact the current High Priest, Roly Bones, is said to perform his out-of-offices diligently despite suffering from a wet weak end.

Sadly, the popularity of Yahtzee began to wane slightly from the 80s onwards with the introduction of campsite games-rooms and arcades. The followers of Yahtzee abhor these (and the practice of having televisions or games consoles in caravans) as they distract from the proper practice of regular worship.

Yahtzeeites believe that when they die they will go to the "Last Resort" where there is eternal sunshine…

...and a 5 star hotel. ✶

TEQUILA

Goddess   of Regret

When life gives you lemons, then you need to find Tequila... ...and salt. Originating amongst an ancient Central American civilisation, Tequila may be the only holy spirit you can bottle. It is a very friendly religion. Every other follower is your besht mate in the whole damn world and you love them man.

Tequila (or Mezcal in the ancient tongue), was appropriated by the Catholics as Santa Margarita, her feast coinciding with Shrove Tuesday, (as in don't forget the Lemon on Santa Margarita Day). Her sacred animal is the Tequila Mockingbird.

Her temple houses a large distillery surrounded by picturesque gardens of spiky agave plants. The air is filled with the sound of the faithful chanting the mantra "Lick, Swallow, Suck". Visitors can obtain (in return for an offering) a bottle of Tequila's sacred libation to take away or consume right there. The floor is pocked with innumerable dents from where thousands of pilgrims have passed out over the centuries. As the saying goes, "One Tequila, two Tequila, three Tequila, FLOOR!".

It is said that the spirit of Tequila has many mystical powers. These include the ability to turn a dog into a fox and the power to make you believe that you are an Adonis when naked. Tequila also has an aspect as a fertility goddess.

In this role she does not so much promote conception, as she prevents effective contraception. It is estimated that around 15% of the world's current population owe their existence to Tequila.

Each bottle of Tequila's holy spirit contains a sacred worm. It is said that after three shots of sacrament the sacred worm will start to speak to you. Sadly it will only speak utter bollocks, but it will still make more sense than the average politician. So drink deep, sit back, and listen to it's distilled wisdom.

These very special worms are bred in the temple where they are raised on a diet of a special alcoholic spirit which is flavoured by placing a mummified human corpse in the bottle.

The worms have to be continually pickled for a year before being allowed out to utter their homilies. During this process the worms have to be very careful not to consume the mummy itself as it may make them hallucinate.

The Tequilan's have an ancient calendar but it is incomplete. Her scholars figured it wouldn't be the end of the world if they never finished it. ✖

EUROS

KNOWN TO THE ROMANS
AS BORACIC

God of Money one does not have

In his origin story Euros was created by Karma-Ron, who abandoned him shortly after his birth. He was picked up and raised by May (the anthropomorphic personification of corn fields) who tried in vain to help him overcome his psychological issues of abandonment and to grow up to be both strong and stable.

Euros became a prodigal son who spurned his supportive extended family. He ambivalently rejected them when he was deceived into believing that the relationship cost him more than he gained from it by the demons Borriz and Gové. The argument over the terms of this separation continued for years, until the patience of his kin was exhausted and they threw him out of the main house to live in the extension. In this isolation he was taunted by the ignorant opinions of the three "Ghosts of Dreams that Never Were". These three malevolent spirits are individually named "Pierced Organ", "Hatie Cockpins" and "Jerkoff Greased-Hog".

The temples of Euros ring with raised voices. They are of somewhat variable construction quality, and some wings are held together with strained red tape. Every time they try to conduct repairs, someone breaks it. On the altar sit 22 sealed and numbered red boxes, a telephone and Noel Edmunds. At the other end of the temple sits a blessed bovine called the "Ber Cow". Should things get too rowdy in the temple, this beast will low loudly. Making a noise that sounds a bit like "Oooooorder!"

During rituals at Euros' temples, a libation of tea is poured in offering and then the remainder shared amongst the congregation. Tea is considered sacred to Euros because tea leaves. The liturgy will then be read out. This may seem to be nonsense at first, but don't worry. The officiating priest will repeat it more and more slowly and increasingly loudly UNTIL YOU UNDERSTAND. At the end of the rite the priest will bid farewell to his flock with the words "See EU later". His sacred texts were displayed on the sides of political campaign buses, until people realised they were bollocks.

You can only join the priesthood of Euros if you have a protruding navel. You must also have a stoic philosophy and be capable of cussedly sticking with a course of action, even when everyone else can see that it is a path to destruction. Vestments are very important to the priests, and each will have a changing cabinet to facilitate the necessary sartorial standard. Debating is a key skill for a priest of Euros to have. They are capable of arguing for years with nothing resolved. When not on duty, they do enjoy kicking back with a game of chequers.

Be very wary of incurring the wrath of Euros. When angered he is capable of raining a ferment of bile down on his hapless target. These tempests are known as "Farages", and they are capable of destroying a man in two shakes. Sadly, Euros is rarely a wise or fair judge, and has often wrongly attacked the victim of the situation.

The great festival of Euros is held on ~~29th March~~. ~~31st October~~. 31st January? ✂

FLŒLLA

Goddess of Children's Television

The epitome of vivacity and grace, Floella imparts the gifts of laughter, imagination and wisdom to children and the eternally young at heart. She is assisted in this by her friends; The Holy Humpty, Theodore Maximus, Theodore Minimus, Jemima the Ragged Angel and Katoo the Carnivorous Cockatoo.

Her scriptures tell of their travails and triumphs in overcoming the evil infant-demon "Hamble the Terrifier", who is eventually defeated by "Poppy the Less Scary". With a knitting needle. Up the bum.

Here's her temple, here's the door. 1, 2, 3, 4. There's a round window, a square window and an arched window*. Which window will we look through today?

Her temple opens every day at 11am. Inside her temple her worshippers play, dress up, sing, dance, hear stories, draw pictures with big fat crayons or run around and around going, "neenaw neenaw neenaw neenaw" whilst pretending to be a fire engine.

There are many large empty cardboard boxes lying around. It is important to know that they are not cardboard boxes. They are castles, and spaceships, and racing cars and submarines, and houses, and bob sleighs.

The walls are adorned with thousands of proudly hung children's paintings of Floella and her friends (usually depicting her with six fingers, an ear on her forehead and LOTS of love.) The floor is adorned with glitter and cockatoo poo**.

The worshippers are overseen by kindly priests and priestesses who wear brightly coloured robes. They have all trained hard for at least three years at Play School to enter the priesthood.

Mounted high on the wall of Floella's temple is The Big Clock. When the little hand points to eleven and the big hand points to twenty three, then it's time pack your toys away and to say goodbye until another day.

In 1988 they attempted to close and sell off the temple of Floella due to cutbacks in religious funding. It was briefly replaced by a replacement Playbus service.

Floella has ascended to overseeing the "Playschool of Lords". Which is far less mature and civilised than a room full of three year olds.

**More recently constructed temples also have a triangular window.*
***And the blood of Johnny Ball.*

THERMOS

God of Stewed Tepid Drinks

Thermos watches over all who must take their refreshment on the go and on the cheap. He is said to have a luke warm personality and to be frequently more stewed than is good for him. Despite all this he will still fight for your right to par tea.

Thermos has no temples. He is worshipped on beaches, park benches and building sites. He is perhaps most loudly praised at public events where his sacred vessels make excellent stealth whiskey camouflage.

In mythology Thermos rides across the heavens in a motorcycle with a sidecar to the celestial viewpoint, where he has a cup of tea and a nice sit down. The origin of Thermos is steeped in mystery and originates way back in antiquitea. He is said to have been there when the Mesopotamian potters first threw tea pots on their new fangled wheels.

The priests of Thermos can be recognised by their wearing of the ceremonial knotted hankie and the holy tartan travel rug. They are a closely knit brotherhood who tend to live an insulated life. Their motto is "Fraternitea, Sanctitea, Cuppatea". Should you decide to join them, you are likely to form many brew-tea-ful friendships. There are subsects of Thermos who eschew the traditional tea in favour of coffee, cocoa or tomato soup, but these are largely accepted and tolerated by the mainstream faith. The current High Priest of Thermos is the 6th Earl Grey of Theday.

They also have accredited oracles within the faith. These diviners use Tasseomancy, mainly to advise you on how to improve your sex life. You can't do better than going to an Oracle of Thermos when you need some PG tips. The worst possible omen you can receive is the shape of a crimson flask in the tea leaves. This grim portent is know as the Flask of the Red Death. You can always tell who has seen this dreaded sign, as they will leave the oracle looking very poe faced.

Dwelling with each oracle of Thermos there is a butler-priest who's role is to ensure your flask is spotlessly clean. Dressed in an immaculate black suit, he will greet you when you arrive at the door and take your tannin stained chalice from you. As you depart he will return it to you in sparkling condition. This servant of the faith is known as the Flask Jeeves.

When followers of Thermos are forced to confront their mortalitea, they believe they will go to their eternal rest in the mythical land of Twinings, provided they have lived a virtuous life. Those who have lived a decadent, hedonistic life of frequenting cafes and coffee shops will be sucked down into the dark underworld of Typhoo. At a Thermosian funeral, the ashes of the deceased are interred in a brightly coloured tartan flask and buried in the earth. The handy plastic cup atop the flask is used to ceremonially dig and fill in the grave. Very, very slowly.

Beware of offending Thermos. When enraged, he visits his wrath on puny mortals by magically filling their hot drinks with shards of glass. He is the arch enemy of the sea witch "Starbuck". ✄

SENNA

Goddess of Regular Occurrences

Consistency is the watchword of Senna the goddess of regular occurrences. Her followers will visit her temple daily without fail, sometimes more often. Here they make their offerings smoothly and without obstruction. The religion was founded around 700CE, by an extremely pedantic philosopher who was known as "The Anal Bede".

Her temple is divided into individual stalls or "Meditation Pods" where worshippers will cogitate in companionable solitude. Each pod is equipped with it's own throne of contemplation, sacred scroll and library of faith reading such as "Oh Wally, Where Art Thou?" and "The Garfield Philosophy". Her sacred scrolls are soft, strong, very, very long and perforated into handy sheets. The back of each meditation pod door is adorned with a small sculpture of an angry drunken octopus (which doubles as a coat hook).

The rows of Meditation Pods open out onto a space equipped with basins for ritual cleansing. Unlike other faiths where one cleanses oneself before attending a shrine, worshippers of Senna will wash as they leave.

If you are in need and wrestling to achieve the desired ruminative state, the priests or priestess will give you a chalice of sanctified prune juice, to ease the passing of your spiritual suffering. More substantial refreshments are available from the temple café, such as fig rolls and bran muffins.

Famous thinkers throughout history have found relief and inspiration in the temple of Senna. Sir Isaac Newton was once famously visited when he was stuck trying to simultaneously devise his laws of motion and trying to pass an eight egg omelette. In the end, with the help of Senna, he worked both of them out with a pencil.

Her temple is gloriously decorated by the art, verse and musings that thousands of pilgrims have inscribed on the walls over the years. Such as the famous lines, said to be by Lord Byron:

"There I sat, broken hearted,
I'd paid a penny and only farted,
My tightened lips in prayer a-quivered,
and Praise be to Senna! I was delivered." ✤

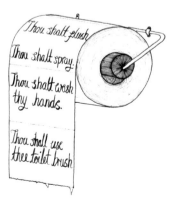

PERINEUM

God of the Middle World
(Stuck between heaven and a very dark place)

Neither one thing nor the other in all aspects. His followers believe that the path to true happiness is indecision. If you never resolve anything, no one will ask you to do anything ever again and inner peace will be achieved. Pain and suffering occur when others force you to choose. His most famous hymn is "Meh, meh, meh, meh, s'alright 's'pose".

All temples of Perineum are of a tall and unstable design. Having been built by committee, they have floors and floors of flaws. Perineum's temples each have two doors. One rosy coloured and one of rusty hue with a pink wall in between. The most profound act of worship in this faith is to hover around the two doors to the temple nervously for an hour but never go in. If one does go inside, you will find there are no pews to sit on. Instead there are rows and rows of Theological Fences upon which one must perch.

Honouring your parents is a key tenet of the faith of Perineum. One room in every temple is dedicated to be the Chapel of Episiotomy. In this sanctuary, behind a torn curtain, worshippers give grateful thanks for the sacrifices their mothers have made on their behalf. This is an emotional experience and supplicants are often moved to tears. Offerings of spools of surgical suture thread are traditionally left on soft cushions on the altar.

Perineum's sacred animal is the common domestic cat. His temples always have a resident clowder. They display the epitome of indecisiveness as they stand at the temple door asking to go out, and then come in, and go out, and come in, and go out and come in.

The faith of Perineum has several historically significant sacred sites around the world. Perhaps the most famous of these is found in the English county of Barseshire, near the quaint village of Tinter. Here the Biffin Bridge stretches across a gorge between Cuntock Hills leading to the ancient Temple of Perineum d'Brexit. This temple has a massive split running right down the middle of the building, and three large extensions (at the last count). The temple complex is enclosed by a convenient six foot deep ditch.

One of the roles of the Priesthood of Perineum is to dispense justice. Unfortunately, no trials are ever resolved. Every single one ends in a hung jury. Never go out for a restaurant meal with a group of Perineum worshippers. Firstly, your fellow diners may never make it to the restaurant, many casualties will end up forever trapped in their dressing rooms trying to select the perfect outfit. Even if they do manage to arrive at the restaurant before 6pm, you still won't have ordered by midnight. This is probably where the dark rumours about cannibalism in the distant history of the faith stem from. Followers of Perineum never plan their lives, they just lurch from indecision to indecision.

The most famous ancient Perineal philosopher, Maybemonides, once said, "Indecision is preferable to the terror of a wrong decision."

In mythology Perineum is a somewhat sensitive deity, that feels like they never get enough attention. Traditionally one has to be careful not to offend Perineum. One slip and you will be in the deep brown.

HOUMOUS

God of Dips

Houmous is the deity to get your party started on a Saturday night. As you enter his temple you will see niches to either side of the door holding bowls of Tzatziki. Use some of this to make the sign of the Benevolent Breadstick on your forehead as you cross the threshold.

In the Temple grounds a plethora of sesame, chick peas and garlic are lovingly grown. Just beyond the grounds is the ranch where the sacred herd of yoghurt cows roam and graze a lush paddock. The temple itself is made of cut crystal, and is divided into sections to house different flavours of the faith.

Inside the beat is always dropping and the lights are always low. Worshippers may be reclining on chaise, performing ritual dances or be engaged in deep theological discussion about the nacho versus the crisp. All the while the neophytes circle the room bearing laden platters of nibbles and bowls of delicious sauces.

Whispers speak of secret orgiastic rites, held in the inner sanctum, where the participants paint their naked bodies with taramasalata and engage in wild salsa dancing.

The 5 Commandments of Houmous are;
1. Thou shall not double dip.
2. Thou shall not dip meat products when there are vegetarians at the party.
3. Thou shall not buy long life dips in jars unless thou art already really drunk or thy fridge be broken.
4. Thou shall wash thy hands.
5. Thou shall use a cover during fly season.

Worshippers of Houmous believe that if they live a life of virtue according to these commandments, when they die they will go to an eternal paradise known as "The Thousand Islands". If you transgress the commandments you will be damned to eternity in a dismal underworld where the only things to eat are low fat plain yoghurt and celery. The high priest of Houmous is called the Baba Ghanoush.

Houmous is known amongst his pantheon as a particularly foul mouthed deity. He is always coming out with loads of crudités. He is accompanied everywhere by "The Cheesehog", a terrifying minor deity of children's birthday parties. ✤

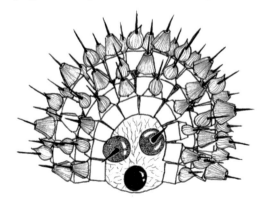

PATHOS

God of Internet Hugs

Pathos is the God of remote love and good wishes when the going gets tough. He is the God of cute animal gifs and that cat that is "hanging in there baby". The walls of the temple of Pathos are decorated with inspirational and motivational quotes superimposed on atmospheric images of the ocean. Pathos' power is strengthened by his celestial familiar "Likeus", who takes the form of an insatiable wolf.

The followers of Pathos are people who "just can't even" right now. They are lead by the priesthood of Pathos, who are skilled cryptographers. They create elaborate and abstruse coded messages designed to generate attention and sympathy from the general following, but only be clear in their meaning to one target individual. Some of the greatest examples, which have been recorded in his sacred text "The Book of Faces", include;

"Can't trust no one can you,"
"At the hospital,"
"Sick of fake friends. It's just me and the kids from now on,"
and the brief but poignant,
"FML"

Sadly, the "Book of Faces" can be hard to read for a neophyte, as the fluid approach to spelling and grammar can make things a little hard to follow. When they are not engaged in ciphering or leading worship, the Priests of Pathos generally like to go fishing for cats. This provides both recreation and emotional sustenance. However, whenever a disaster occurs somewhere in the world they will leap into action to send thoughts and prayers. The sect is headed by a high priestess who holds the title of "The Drama Queen".

Once a year a great festival of Pathos is held where epic theatrical productions are staged. The great writers compete to stage the best tragedy play. The performing company is comprised of a few principal actors, who will deliver lines loaded with mysterious snippets of information from behind masks with frozen expressions. These traditional masks portray the six different reactions humans are capable of having. They are called Likey, Lovey, Laughy, Wowee, Weepy and Angry. Behind the main players stand a chorus who beg for more details from the background. The plays are judged by a committee chosen by lot from the audience. The winning playwright is awarded a ceremonial giant stirring spoon carved from ivy wood. Perhaps the most famous playwright to honour Pathos with his work was S'upocles, best known for his play "Antagonize".

(Most people won't read this entry but, if you share the word of Pathos I'll know who really reads my book. Put a 🐋 on your status for the next hour to raise awareness of Pathos.) �֎

P.S. You okay Hun? PM me.

BEROCCAS

God of Vitamins

Beroccas is always depicted as the buffed epitome of health and vitality, and he's really, really proud of it. He is the twin brother of Dioralyte - God of Minerals and Electrolytes.

A typical rite at Beroccas' temple begins with the chanting of the RDAs, followed by a 30 minute sermon about Beroccas gym and running regime. There will be singing of sacred songs such as the well known favourites "Amazin' Riboflavin" or "Thiamin be the Glory". At the climax of the ritual, the officiating priest will drop the fizzy tablet into the water to make it holy, and then it is shared by his followers as a libation.

The air of the temple hangs thick with a mist of perspiration. Three of the walls are lined with wall to ceiling mirrors, the fourth is a plate glass window which looks out onto the street. This way, any unbelievers walking past will be awed by the majesty of physiques of the faithful at prayer. The aisles are filled with rows of exercise bikes which spin prayer wheels. Each worshipper carries a small prayer towel, which must be used to wipe the seat clean of their pious perspiration.

Members of the cult of Beroccas are required to attend a form of confessional every week where they must download their fitness tracker watch data for scrutiny by the High Priest. Those who have earned an insufficient number of badges are punished by being picked last for all team games for the next week.

The Beroccan Games are held every four years in a different city around the world. At these games believers compete in athletic events to win a place in the Priesthood. Only the finest specimens of health and prowess are admitted. They compete naked. Even though no one asked them to.

Beroccas is sometimes prayed to by the hungover, desperately promising lifestyle reform in exchange for relief. It is said by his true acolytes that these prayers will fall on deaf ears and they would do better praying to Cholesterolia - Goddess of Fry-Ups.

Followers of Beroccas believe that when they die, they'll be over 100 and still look foxy.

SITHEE

God of South Yorkshire

Nah then! Sithee is the God of the desolate industrial wasteland* that stretches from Chesterfield to Wakefield. He represents this benighted county with a Thorne in its side. He is the county's own God. Sithee is a deity of many avatars. He has died and been re-incarnated at least 25 times. With each death more dramatic and poignant than the last. He is one of the few deities to be a martyr to his own faith. Between each incarnation, his priesthood will form a circle and chant the word "Bastard" over and over until he is born again. Sithee's sacred animal is a mighty water serpent, which likes to coil in t'bath. He is sometimes depicted with his ceremonial weapon, used for stabbing his enemies in the guts, called the "Tripedent".

Sithee's priesthood maintain his temples and conduct the "Reyts" of worship. The music for these rituals is supplied by a live brass band playing traditional South Yorkshire tunes, such as "Don't You Want Me Baby" and "Disco 2000". For occasions of great gravitas, they will play the hoviest of hymns, Largo from Dvorak's New World Symphony. At the climax of the Reyt a cup of tea is shared amongst the congregation as a kind of communion. A proper Yorkshire brew is made in the ceremonial tea pot. Which is never washed. The oldest of these ceremonial tea pots has such thick tannin deposits inside that it barely holds a thimbleful of water.

There are four temples of Sithee, located in Sheffield, Rotherham, Barnsley and Doncaster. One does not simply walk into a Temple of Sithee. The best way to get there is by Eagle Cars. Don't try to get there on the 120 bus. It will only get you to Halfway (and you'll be robbed if you try to get there on the 52 as it has Crookes on it). You can't use your own car to get there as, strangely, there is no parkin nearby.

Every year Sithee demands a tribute. One night each summer, unwary Offcumdens are herded into t'Wicker Ski Village, and the whole thing is set ablaze. It is then rebuilt ready for next year's ritual burning. One year, Diana Rigg was nearly accidentally ignited. The priesthood were momentarily confused by her theatrical R.P. English and put her into the rattan chalet. As the flames started to take hold around her, one of the priests sarcastically asked the sacrifices "All reyt?". When Diana answered "Ah. Not s'bad." She was immediately rescued.

The church is renowned for being inclusive of the LGBTQ+ community. One day the message board outside the temple read "Sithee loves shirt-lifters", and from that point onwards the gay following grew. The church leaders decided to keep very quiet about the fact that they originally put up the message to try and get a corporate sponsorship from Farrow's Mushy Peas.

The church of Sithee runs a dating advice service, where young men can learn the art of elegant chat up lines. Amongst the tried and tested Yorkshire chat up lines you can learn are, the passionate "Brace thi'ssen Lass" and the more casual "Wake up". The church also run a charitable emergency ambulance service. You can recognise their ambulances by their distinctive sirens which go, "Dee-da, dee-da, dee-da, dee-da".

Should you decide to be initiated into the church of Sithee, be prepared to undergo a strange and dark Reyt. First one will be anointed with a special blend of Henderson's Relish and River Don Water. Then one has to hold a ferret in one's trousers whilst pouring molten steel from a crucible and forging it to make a Sheffield Steel knife. Only the most dedicated, steady handed and pain oblivious neophytes make it to full membership. If you make it however, you earn the privilege of calling all the other priests "Love". ✂

*No. You can't see any rolling purple moors, dramatic views, secluded wooded valleys, elegant stately homes or picturesque parks. It's all an optical illusion in your mind. Now keep quiet about it. If you tell anyone, they'll just think you're mad.

BANKSIA

Goddess of Modern Art

The Goddess Banksia was created when the Green Fairy of the Bohemian Revolution was splattered against the windscreen of Jackson Pollock's speeding car. Banksia watches over all Modern, Contemporary and Conceptual Artists. If you have to ask whether or not it is art, then it falls under the province of Banksia. Unlike other gods (which you may be encouraged to "find") NO ONE WANTS YOU TO FIND BANKSIA. The mystery will always be more enigmatic than the answer.

The first time you see a temple of Banksia, the radical architecture may make you wonder whether the building is a work of art or just still under construction. Above the main entrance the letters W.T.F. are carved into the stonework. Most of the rooms inside the temple are either light, airy galleries or studios. The galleries are the only areas where the general public are allowed. (The Security Avant Guards control access.) The private studios are cluttered rats nests that "are exactly the way we like it so don't you dare touch a thing". Each temple of Banksia also has a room where devotees can go for comfort when they are drowning in depressing thoughts that their art is contrived and unoriginal. This is called the Negative Space. The final room you might visit in the temple is the smallest one. A post-modernist bathroom installation known as the Po-Mo (by R. Mutt). Whatever you do, do not actually use it. It's not plumbed in and it has a price tag which means it will be the most expensive penny you ever spend.

The Priesthood of Banksia proudly wear their official robes of office, which look like paint streaked old shirts. They always have unruly manes of hair, for of the hundred or so brushes that each priest owns, not one of them is a hairbrush. (Or a sweeping brush.) When one stands within about 50 meters of a priest of Banksia, one can detect their distinctive perfume, a blend of linseed oil and turpentine. The current High Priest in residence is Mr Art Majors. Because an artist's work tends to increase in value after their death, the thing a Banksian priest dreads most is seeing their doctor coming into the temple and buying all of their paintings.

When the mortal coil finally ends, the church of Banskia offers unconventional funerary services. These are open to all who wish to achieve aesthetic immortality. Their firm of funeral directors Van Hagens & Hirst are amazingly popular. You can be your own beautiful memento mori! If you attend a Banksian funeral, it is important to show the proper respect for the deceased by speaking in dead pantones.

The church of Banksia is not typically a wealthy one. The principal revenue raiser is the sale of the artwork they produce. Sadly, when they do sell a piece, they usually make less profit than the person who framed it. The Monochromist sect are the only acolytes to actually generate a reliable income for the faith. As a money-maker they produce those paint colour cards you can pick up at the DIY shop. They also sometimes name new colour shades using the rejected working titles for their own artwork. This is why there is a shade of bluish green non drip gloss called Poseidon's Vomit. Any surplus income is invested in public arts schemes. Their next planned project is the building of a giant steel protractor at the side of the A1 near Gateshead (working title "The Angle of the North").

Should you decide to visit a temple of Banksia for a little enlightenment one rainy Sunday afternoon, be very careful what you say whilst inside. If anyone is heard to utter the blasphemous words "Huh! I could have done that." in her temple, one of the priests will thwack them around the head with a large, heavy marble tablet inscribed with the words "Yeah. But you didn't!"

Acknowledgements

Thank you to all the patrons who helped
Idol Scribblings—The Book
become a reality by pre-ordering their copy.

Teresa Lee
Michael Lee
Janet Hudson
Kris Hudson-Lee
Dr Pascal Harper
Heather Harper
Katherine Lynn
Philip G Lort
Nick Ward
Jen Titley
Andy Bolton
Richard Jackson
Paula Turner
John Kennard
Alex Smith
Kay Healy
Barry Healy
Cis Heaviside
Steve Carthy
Wendy Barrows
Carey Anne Boyce
Rebecca Stothard
Sam Whiting

Stephen Jackson
Fury
Maire McPoland
Gillian Taylor
Kate Karnage
Slapper
Dr Gareth Wilden
Di Oxley-Wilden
Sarah Allison
Robin Lawrence
Amber Lee
Adrian Waite
Elaine Waite
Barbara Chambers
Martin Thiselton
Jackie Thiselton
Adam Broadhurst
Larry Brennan
Andrew Lee
Anthony Carroll
Moira Varley
Jennifer Lane
Christopher Lane

This book could not have been produced without the
suggestions, creativity, wit, support and encouragement of

"The Idol Scribblings Hive Mind"

Wendy Barrows	Adam Tomlinson	Fury
Dr Pascal Harper	Dr Garth Wilden	Moira Varley
John Kennard	Phil Hyde	Maire McPoland
Carey Anne Boyce	Dave Redford	Bryony Nightingale
Ju Haynes	Steve Carthy	Di Oxley-Wilden
Adam Broadhust	Alexandra Smith	Pete Bailey
Teresa Lee	Kumi Chavda	Annie Hancock
Nigel Harper	Ju Haynes	Josh Matkin
Sarah Allison	Heather Harper	Philip G Lort
Ken Page	Chris Wiley	Dr Amber Syed
Janet Hudson	Clare Griffin	Richard Jackson
Jen Titley	Stephen Jackson	Cis Heaviside
Xander Kennard	Paul O'Neill	Charlotte Creasey
Carrie-May Mealor	Barbara Chambers	Kevin Wiltshire
Kris Hudson-Lee	Larry Brennan	Mike Lee
Rebecca Stothard	Carol Overrill	Robin Lawrence
Jerome Perks	Jerome Perks	Kieron Philips
Anthony Carroll	Naomi Louise Baker	Alan Boyce
James R Turner	Heather Faulkner	Sam Whiting
Dr Will Bayley	Kate Rennie	Lana May
Jake Cosford	Keith Scholfield	Kate Karnage

I feel very blessed to count you clever buggers
as my friends.

HANNAH

Goddess of Terrible Puns

About the Author

Hannah is what you might call one of England's typical eccentrics. In keeping with the random and useless theme of this book, here are 10 random and useless facts about her.

�֍ Her first published writing was a contribution to the Viz Profanisaurus, for which she was paid the princely sum of one Knackersack Pencil.

✖ She has slept overnight in more castles than the Most Haunted team have run screaming out of, and once went down to the pub with the giant key to Skipton Castle gate hung from her belt.

✖ She once lived in a tent for four months to get the chance to see a total solar eclipse.

✖ She toured the USA with a band at the age of 17 in a bus with rainbows, suns, moons, stars and flames painted on it.

✖ She taught science to the children of South Yorkshire for 15 years and still lives. So do most of the children.

✖ She was once featured in an article in Morris Minor Owner Magazine. The accompanying photograph showed her in fifteenth century dress with her billhook strapped to the roof of a Black 1967 1000 Saloon.

✖ She has eaten jellyfish. It tasted like fishy jelly.

✖ She is the lead singer of the folk band Ethryll. Their most popular song is a musical rant about potholes.

✖ She was once on the local TV news in the "and finally" section. The cameras caught a knight in a full suit of armour pinching her bum, and her slapping him and knocking him 10 feet backwards.

✖ She is not very good at carpentry. She once made a nest box that remained rejected by the birds for years. In the end her Grandpa put a little sign on it that said "No Poll Tax". Which answers your question of "Where does she get it from?"